NO FLO
ON A
SAILOR'S GRAVE

*Shipwrecks of
Kinsale and Courtmacsherry*

Jerome Lordan

Old Head Press

Title:
No flowers on a Sailors Grave:
Shipwrecks of Kinsale and Courtmacsherry

Author: Jerome Lordan

Published by Old Head Press

Front cover courtesy of Kevin Dwyer

Design & Print by Star Creative
part of *The Southern Star* newspaper

Contents

Preface

The *Lusitania* is the most famous shipwreck off the coast of Cork. The Cunard liner and its passengers and crew were deliberate casualties of war, most shipwrecks were victims of the weather and bad luck. In fact, the recent shipwreck of the Dutch training vessel, the *Astrid,* near Kinsale, is far more typical – reminding us just how dangerous the seas were, and still are, off the southwest coast of Ireland. In the days of sail and steam the southern coast of Ireland - with Queenstown and Cork Harbour at its centre - was a popular rendezvous point for ships beginning and ending the transatlantic crossing. However, in bad weather many ships ended up instead wrecked on the rocky shores of Kinsale and Courtmasherry.

In this book Jerome Lordan (MA, UCC) provides a valuable record of the known shipwrecks in the area during the modern period. In doing so, he has located many primary accounts and original illustrations and has deployed these to good effect. Above all, he has brought his own local specialist knowledge to bear on the subject. It is his knowledge of local people, local places and local sea conditions, his expertise as a mariner and indeed his eye for a good story that makes this book. As a result, it stands as an important contribution, not just to local history, but also to the burgeoning maritime history of Ireland.

Hiram Morgan
School of History
University College
Cork
June 2014

Acknowledgements

To the now deceased Peninsula people who inspired me without they or I knowing it.

To the late Francie Dempsey whose knowledge and love of native place and placenames was one my greatest inspirations. I feel duly obliged to pass on the knowledge that he imparted to me, particularly in relation to placenames.

Ted and Dan Manning of Garrylucas West, at whose fireside on the White Strand tales of shipwrecks and sea lore were discussed till the small hours of the morning.

To Eugene Gillen who always nurtured my interest in all things local with regard to the past.

To Mick O Sullivan who used to go fishing with me in a punt that I inherited from my uncle Tim until I was old enough to take it out on my own. Mick had a great knowledge of the perils that surround the shore on the east side of the Head as well as the colloquial names in the native tongue for every type of fish and every sunken rock.

To Tadgh Bawn, Ger Forde, Frankie Bowen, Mor Calnan, Bill O'Connell and all the older generation who sat around the fire in 'An Doras Breac' and recalled tales of yore.

To my parents who made sure that I got a good education (which at the time I had no interest in) and always supported me.

To Jennifer for all the support, patience, help and technological expertise in putting this work together. It would not have been possible without her.

To Shane Lehane of Heritage Management in Stiofán Naofa who gave me every encouragement and convinced me to further my academic pursuits at UCC. His advice was the best I ever got and to him I am eternally grateful.

To all my former colleagues at UCC, students and lecturers who inspired me through their own achievements – they helped me along my journey.

To Hiram Morgan, my supervisor at UCC, who first planted the seed of this publication by suggesting that I publish a piece on the *Pearl of Gloucester* shipwreck. His critical evaluation was much appreciated.

To Dan McCarthy of the *Examiner* archives who was very supportive with sourcing information.

To Richard Forrest and Kieran Wyse at the County Library who were always helpful and accommodating.

To Brian Magee and his colleagues of the Cork City Archives in Blackpool who patiently assisted me in sourcing material.

To Dorothy Convery of Carrigline Bookshop for reading and re-reading this manuscript.

To Michael O' Brien of Butlerstown who is an authority on the Cardiff Hall to whom I am eternally grateful for his assistance.

To Tony Twomey of the Office of Public Works, who was always willing to share his vast knowledge of the underwater world.

To my good friend Dolly O'Reilly of Sherkin Island for being my sounding board with advice on formation of this book.

To Mick O'Rourke of www. Irishshipwrecks.com who was so generous with guiding me towards what I needed to find.

To Ann and Graham Ferguson of Ocean Addicts who always kept me up to speed on underwater sightings.

To my good friend fisherman Shane Murphy for all our discussions on underwater obstacles and his help with position fixing.

To Tony Bocking a stalwart of the Kinsale Historical Society for our regular morning exchanges of historical information on the Pier Road.

To John Thuillier for being so generous in sharing his knowledge and information.

To Paddy O' Sullivan of Bandon – Lusitania expert extraordinaire who was always so enthusiastic to share his knowledge.

To John Collins for so generously offering fabulous underwater photos.

To Michael Prior for his expertise in photography and for his amazing efforts in capturing the ultimate image.

To Igan Gillan for his mapping expertise and patience.

To Rob Jacob for his artistic expertise and his fabulous hand-drawn charts.

To Sean Mahon and Alan Tobin of the *Southern Star* for their invaluable advice in formatting.

To Ian Killick at the UK Hydrographic Office for all his assistance.

To Deirdre O'Sullivan for her proof reading.

To Alannah Hopkin for her proof reading.

To Dónal O'Sullivan for his final proof reading.

To Bobby Nash of Latitude Kinsale for his guidance in accessing charts.

My thanks also to Billy Lynch, Brian Perrot, Dermot Collins, Diarmuid Kingston, Gerry McCarthy, John O'Dwyer, John O'Gorman, Mary Whelton, Michael Arundel, Pádraig O'Donovan, Pat Collins, Vincent Downing, Captain Phil Devitt, Peggy Connolly, Chris Guy, Eamon O'Neill, Billy Fleming, Mark Gannon, Mia Kovacs, Rachel Barrett, Don O'Herlihy, Barry Moloney, Ciarán Dempsey, Mícheál Hurley, Leila Cotter, Connie Kelleher and J.P. Downing.

Biography

Jerome Lordan's family has lived at the Old Head of Kinsale for generations on his maternal (Dempsey) side. He attended the Old Head National School, St Peter's College, Wexford and Rochestown College, Cork. He worked as a commercial fisherman in New Zealand, Australia and Cornwall and all round Ireland during a 28-year career. He has been the owner of Kinsale Harbour Cruises since 2003. After studying Heritage Management at Coláiste Stiofán Naofa, Cork, Jerome completed a B.A. in Archaeology and Celtic Civilization at University College Cork, where he was awarded an M.A. in Local History with First Class Honors in 2012 for his thesis on the local placenames of the Old Head. His work is inspired by his deep love of place and his knowledge of local topography, folklore and oral tradition.

Figures

Glossary

Nautical terms:

1 Fathom .... 6 Feet.
1 Cable .... .0.1 Nautical Mile.
1 Knot....................... 1 Nautical mile (1.852km)
Sea Fencibles............ Local based naval reserve
 Fast........................... Trawl caught on the bottom.
Mis-stayed................ This means a sailing craft has failed in an attempt to come about.
Broad Reach............. Running with the wind on the vessel's quarter.
Beam Reach .... Running with the wind on the vessel's beam.
Stranded................... Went ashore.
Schooner.................. A fore and aft rigged vessel, two or more masts, foremast shorter than main.
Brigantine................ A two masted vessel, square rigged on the foremast, fore and aft rigged on main.
Lugger .... A fishing boat, two or more masts, with lug sails.
Drifter....................... A fishing vessel engaged in drift netting.
Smack........................ A traditional fishing boat.
Brig........................... A two masted square rigged vessel.
Barque...................... A sailing vessel with three or more masts. Fore and aft rigged only on the aftermast.
Pilot Cutter .... A small single-masted boat, with two or more headsails and often a bowsprit.
Dandy........................ A sail fishing vessel, usually smack rigged.
Ketch .... A sailing vessel, two masts, forward one is larger, traditionally square rigged.
Galley .... A vessel propelled by rowing, but also carried sails for favourable winds.
Man o' War .... A sailing warship.
Galiot........................ A small galley type of vessel.
Pinnace .... A small ship's boat.

Latitude and Longitude are only given in instances where the close proximity of the wreck is known. The positions given for wrecks in both Kinsale and Courtmacsherry Harbours are for the most part taken from records that state ships were lost in those harbours without giving an exact position. The majority of the other wrecks that were lost and recorded in each of the charts are in known positions. Some shipwrecks do not appear in any of the charts in this book either because their locations are unknown or they are located outside the chart areas (20 or more miles off shore).
Some positions on the charts are only approximate (no co-ordinates given).

Placenames & Irish terms:

Irish language only versions of placenames are given where there is no English version or equivalent of that name, just mere interpretations. Many of these names are nuanced and attempts at translation are often misleading. These are usually found in peripheral areas of the coast, where Irish was the main language. Names given in both Irish and English often have two different names, one that was used by the native Gaelic speaking community and the other used by the English speaking community. Names in English only are the result of the Anglicisation of a place over a long period of time and where the native names are lost.

Badbh and *Morrígan*	Harbingers of impending doom in Irish mythology.
Arthrach Maol	A phantom ship with tattered sails, seen just before a vessel is shipwrecked.
Cuas	Cove
Tráigh	Strand
Faill	Cliff
Carraig	Rock
Bollán	A rounded sunken rock
Faill na Reilig	Cliff of the burial ground.
Leaba Loinge	Bed of the ship.
Cuas na Cnámh	Cove of the bones.
Leabaidh a' Bhád	Bed of the boat.
Cuas na Marbh	Cove of the dead.
Cuas a'Loinge	Cove of the ship.
Cuaisín na nDaoine Báite	Little cove or inlet of the drowned people.
Cuas a'Sasainigh	Cove of the Englishman.
Cuas a'Bhád	Cove of the boats.
Cuas a' Reca	Cove of the wreck.
Rinnplúir	Point of the flour.
Scoth na Loinge	Narrow ridge of the ship.
Droichead na Fían	Bridge of the Fingellans.
Cuas Cannon	Cove or inlet of the cannon.
Poll na Bolg	Hole of the bellows.

Wind and tide:

Spring tide: This occurs when the sun and the moon are nearest to the earth and tidal flow is strongest. This results in very high and very low tides.

Neap tide: This occurs when the sun and the moon are furthest from the earth and tidal flow is weakest. This results in less extreme tides.

High Tide/High water: This occurs every 6 hours before and after a low tide.

Low Tide/Low Water: This occurs every 6 hours before and after a high tide.

Fresh	Force 5 to 7 (21-33 knots)
Gale	Force 8 (34-40 knots)
Strong Gale	Force 9 (41-47 knots)
Storm	Force 10 (48-55 knots)
Violent Storm	Force 11 (56-63 knots)
Hurricane	Force 12 (64 knots)

Introduction

This work is an attempt, in so far as it is possible, to draw up a definitive account of shipwrecks for the area between Oysterhaven and the southeast corner of the Seven Heads. It is written with a mariner's perspective on the various happenings, and also from a well-informed local viewpoint. The original reports were mostly written by people who only had an outsider's view of the area. The author questions these accounts critically from his own unique viewpoint, as a mariner with local knowledge of the rocky coastline and its hazards, placenames and traditional lore.

Prior to the 1850s, little was known of the many wrecks that foundered in the study area. Locational detail was vague, possibly because the people who recorded these events only knew the name of the prominent headlands and ports and knew little or nothing about the many little bays, inlets and reefs that abound across the study area. Often these reports consisted of second- or third-hand information and details were scant. The appearance of local newspapers like the *Cork Examiner* (1841), the *West Cork News & County Advertiser* (1870) and later the *Southern Star* (1889), contributed hugely to better documentation of local affairs. The predecessors of these newspapers, most notably the *Cork Constitution* (1823), were more concerned with the affairs of the various happenings in the wider British Empire than in local affairs.

In the age of sail and before the era of weather forecasting, shipwrecks were so commonplace that they did not make big news. However, with the advent of steam power, superior lighthouses, buoyage systems and advances in navigational equipment, losses at sea decreased considerably. This, however, all changed with the outbreaks of World Wars I and II, when huge casualties again at sea became commonplace. The lesser-known and little-documented losses are contained in chapters on the different centuries. The better-documented losses are given separate or shared chapters, depending on the amount of information available. The chapters are determined by timelines and location for the most part.

A cross-section of different disciplines is used in the study to give it a broader than normal perspective. Contemporary newspaper reports and historical accounts are supplemented by local knowledge of topography, meteorology, archaeology, folklore and placenames – and the invaluable lore gained from the memories of older members of the local community in informal conversations over the years. The role of the local community in providing help and hospitality to shipwrecked seafarers is given full credit, as are the daring and dramatic rescues carried out with rockets and breeches buoy by local coastguards and life-saving units, and later by the voluntary crews of the local lifeboats.

First-hand experience of commercial fishing and recreational diving in the Old Head area, combined with an in-depth knowledge of local topography, casts new light on many puzzles that have remained unsolved for generations. The different disciplines combine to reveal an entirely new picture of the seafaring past of a key landmark of Ireland's southwest coast, and its role in the bigger and dramatically changing picture of international shipping as the age of sail gives way to steam, and local fishing smacks and coasters are joined by the great transatlantic liners.

Chapter I: 1600-1799

Two Spanish vessels were reported lost near Kinsale on the 11 October 1601.[1]

Reported in Kinsale on 18 January 1666 that a vessel of four guns belonging to London and returning from Malaga, with a considerable quantity of wine and other cargo, ran into the Old Head and many of her men drowned.[2]

Adventure: A ship of London lost in a storm near Kinsale on 11 February 1681.[3]
Providence: This Kinsale ship sank in a storm in six fathoms of water in her home port in 1668.[4]

Gainsborough: Originally named *Swallow*, this man o'war of about 120 ft was built in Plymouth in 1653. Lost in Kinsale Harbour on 9 February 1692.

> On entering the harbour at Kinsale she found a transport vessel blocking the main channel, forcing her to enter shallow water where she attempted to anchor. Whilst in the process a rope became foul of her rudder and out of control she went into a sandbank. It was anticipated that at high water she would float free, but several hull planks gave way whilst she was aground and touching the bottom in the shallows, she commenced to fill. The crew were put to work on her main pump which managed to keep the level of water inside her down, but when the pump broke her crew were forced to abandon her as a total loss.[5]

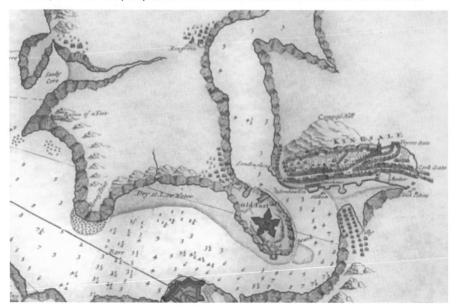

⚓ Fig.1: Late 17th century chart of Kinsale Harbour by Captain Grenville Collins. Courtesy of Barry Moloney & Don O'Herlihy.

---

1   B.T. & R. Larn, *Shipwreck Index of Ireland.*
2   *Corporation Book of Kinsale.*
3   *Historic Shipwrecks of the East & West Cork Coast, Dúchas:* The Heritage Service, 2000.
4   Ibid.
5   D. Hepper, *British Warship Losses in the Age of Sail*, 1650-1859. Rotherfield: Jean Boudriot, 1994.

⚓ Fig.2: Figurehead from the *Swallow* 1692 currently housed in Kinsale Museum. *Courtesy of Kinsale Museum.*

St Albans: Built in 1687 in Deptford, England. This 39m vessel had 50 carriage-mounted cannons. At anchor off the entrance to Kinsale on 8 December 1693, in company with the prize-ship *Virgin*, the wind increased until it reached storm force. Captain Gillman who was onshore accompanied by Captain Hailes of the other ship, attempted to return to his vessel disregarding the obvious physical dangers involved due to rough seas. Just as the ship's pinnace approached the man o' war, it was picked up by a large wave, thrown against the ship's bow, capsized and the occupants thrown into the water. Of the eleven crew and two passengers, only two survived, both captains losing their lives. Her anchor cables later parted and she drove ashore in Sandy Cove where she was wrecked. The remainder of the ship's company was saved apart from one or two men.[6]

⚓ Fig.3 :Sandy Cove Island, many vessels have been lost here, these include the following that have been recorded: *Ruby, Eliza, St Albans,* a corn vessel (name unknown), *Hampden* and *Neptune. Courtesy of Kevin Dwyer.*

Devonshire: This man o'war had her deck blown up by accident on 13 July 1695 in Kinsale Harbour and thirty men were wounded.[7]

Eighteenth-century losses.

The majority of the listings in this chapter come from the Shipwreck Index of Ireland compiled by Bridget Teresa Larn and Richard Larn. This is the most comprehensive list that has been compiled for the coast of Ireland.

6   Ibid.
7   Coleman O'Mahony & Tim Cadogan, 'Shipwrecks on the Cork Coast up to 1810' in *Harbour Lights: Journal of the Great Island Historical Society,* p.21.

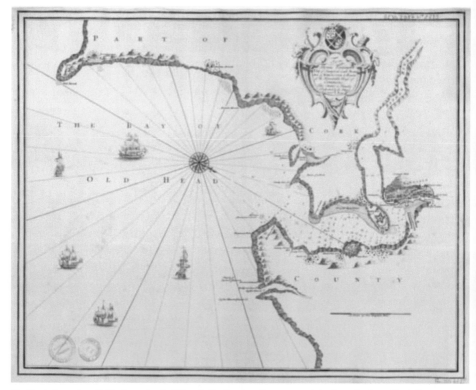

⚓ Fig.4: Seventeenth Century chart of Kinsale Harbour and greater area by Captain Grenville Collins.

John the Baptist: 11 November 1707, reported lost near Kinsale. The captain was Thomas Shurlock.[8]

An unknown galley of 180 tons was lost when it went on the rocks four miles east of Kinsale on 26 February 1729. A ship out of Bordeaux was also abandoned and swamped off the Old Head on the same date.[9]

Friendship: 18 April 1749, reported lost off the Old Head. The master's name was Robinson and the vessel was en route from Cork to Gibraltar.[10]

Concord: February 1750, reported to be stranded near the Old Head. The Bristol ship was bound from Cork to the Bay of Honduras and the master's name was MacNamara. The vessel was reported to be a total loss.[11] The records held at the Dublin Customs House has this loss dated to the previous year (9 February 1749).

Unknown vessel, circa 1750.

8   B.T & R. Larn. *Shipwreck Index of Ireland*. Lloyd's Register-Fairplay Ltd. UK. 2002.
9   www.corkshipwrecks.net
10   B.T & R. Larn. *Shipwreck Index of Ireland*.
11   www.irishshipwrecks.com

A vessel was lured ashore by a false light at Bullen's Bay about 1750. The name of the ship is in doubt as a story tells that that she carried the son of a gipsy who cursed the Bullen family for their deed. All aboard were lost. The curse had sufficient influence that the timbers were not touched for fifty years.[12]

Mary: 15 May 1752, went ashore near the Old Head. The sloop out of Portsmouth was on a voyage from Cadiz to Dublin, carrying a cargo of olive oil and wine. Her captain was Thomas Taylor.[13]

Lovely Betty: 26 January 1753, reported lost in approximate position 51.38N 08.28W south of Kinsale. The sailing vessel out of Liverpool was en route from North Carolina to Liverpool. The captain was named Jackson and most of the crew were drowned.[14]

In a storm a ship from Liverpool was wrecked between the Old Head and Kinsale and several of the crew perished, 7 November 1754.[15]

Santissima Anunciata St Nicholas: 21 November 1758, Spanish vessel lost.

> 'The Santissima Anunciata St Nicholas San Speridien, Captain Demetrio Ulasopula from Bristol to Venice, is lost on a rock near Kinsale, but part of the cargo will be saved'.[16]

Union: Lost at Kilbrittain on 27 December 1763. She was bound for Limerick from her home port of Bristol.[17]

Revenue barge: The Courtmacsherry revenue barge was lost at Kinsale on 26 April 1766. Five boatmen and three women were lost. Two more had returned to the station on horseback.[18]

Unnamed Sloop: Wrecked at the Old Head on 22 December 1767. She was from Padstow bound for Cork.[19]

Ann & Mary: 29 January 1768, reported lost.

> 'Master Stewart, from Casco Bay, is on shore near the Old Head of Kinsale, the ship will be lost, but the cargo saved.[20]

Pompey: 11 April 1768, on a voyage from Antigua to Cork & Bristol, was lost on this date.

> ' The Britannia, master unknown, from Cork, who is arrived at Bristol, brings an account that the ship Pompey, master Songster, from Antigua to Cork & Bristol, run on the spit of rocks to the westward of Kinsale, the 11th instant, and totally lost, and all the crew perished.[21]

Hampden: Wrecked at Sandy Cove on 13 November 1770. Her captain was Dudley.[22]

12   E.J. Bourke. *Shipwrecks of the Irish Coast 1105-1993*. Vol 1, (Power Press, Dublin, 1994), p. 119.
13   B.T & R. Larn. *Shipwreck Index of Ireland*.
14   Ibid.
15   C. O'Mahony & T.Cadogan, 'Shipwrecks on the Co Cork Coast up to 1810' in Harbour Lights No 1, *Journal of The Great Island Historical Society*, 1988, p 28.
16   B.T & R. Larn. *Shipwreck Index of Ireland*.
17   E.J. Bourke, vol 3. p.88.
18   Index to *The Freemans Journal 1763-1771*, prepared by prisoners at Mountjoy Jail circa 1970, in National Library of Ireland.
19   E.J.Bourke. *Shipwrecks of the Irish Coast 1583-2000*, vol 3.
20   B.T & R. Larn. *Shipwreck Index of Ireland*.
21   Ibid.
22   E.J. Bourke, *Shipwrecks of the Irish Coast*, vol 3.

Nancy: 28 November 1771, lost on this date at Bullen's Bay. The vessel was on a voyage from Virginia to Whitehaven. She was carrying a cargo of oil and 800 barrels of coal tar. She struck the rocks and sank; seven of her crew were saved.[23]

French man o'war*:* This ship was sunk after an attack by an English vessel off the Old Head on 8 October 1772.[24]

Neptune: Lost near Sandy Cove on 10 March 1774. The vessel was a coal brig out of Swansea. Only the captain survived.[25]

(Unidentified vessel): 12 July 1774, a French built ship belonging to Liverpool is reported lost near Kinsale. This is not the *Nancy*, also lost on the same date on a voyage from Jamaica to Liverpool. The master of this vessel was named Noble and was also lost nearby.[26] The same source also recounts the story of a western boat laden with salt from Cork to Baltimore that got caught in a storm on 19 October 1775 and was wrecked in a bay on the west side of the Old Head. One of the crew, after a considerable time on a rock which stood out in the sea, was washed off and immediately perished. His companion expected to share his fate, which he would have done, but for the humanity and intrepidity of some of the people on the shore who saved his life at a risk of their own.

Grizzie: 24 November 1775, reported to be stranded off Kinsale. Her cargo of tobacco leaf was saved, but the ship filled in the next tide. The master's name of this Glasgow ship was McKillar and the vessel was bound for Limerick from Glasgow.[27]

Charlotte: Reported lost at Kinsale on 9 February 1776. This was a Bristol ship on a voyage from Jamaica to Bristol. All the crew were saved.[28]

Rialto: Reported to be lost in Kinsale Harbour on 13 December 1776. Ship out of Bristol and on a voyage from Jamaica to Bristol, master Tapscot.[29]

Hibernia: Reported lost near Kinsale Harbour on 4 March 1777. This 130-ton brig was on a voyage from Bristol to Cork. The master's name was Knethell and all the crew were saved.[30]

Boreas: Reported wrecked near Kinsale on 1 January 1778. The master named, Whitfield, and three crew drowned.[31]

Stillorgan: Wrecked attempting to enter Kinsale Harbour on 16 June 1778. The ship went to pieces at the Great Seal and is not listed in Lloyds Register of Ships. She was a 90- gun British warship.[32]

23   B.T & R. Larn. *Shipwreck Index of Ireland*.
24   *Freemans Journal*, January 1770-December 1771.
25   E.J. Bourke, *Shipwrecks of the Irish Coast 1105-1993*, vol 1, and p.120.
26   B.T & R. Larn. *Shipwreck Index of Ireland*.
27   Ibid.
28   Ibid.
29   Ibid.
30   Ibid.
31   Ibid.
32   C. O'Mahony & T. Cadogan, 'Shipwrecks of the Cork Coast up to 1810' .

The location of the placename Great Seal is not known today, however, there are several local placenames in Irish with seal variants incorporated within the name.[33]

There are a couple of possibilities for this location, either at *Carraig na Rón* at south edge of Middle Cove, or *Carraig na Rón* in Bullen's Bay.

A two-masted vessel from Bideford was wrecked on the Farmer Rock in Kinsale Harbour. The master, mate and two hands were lost on 23 December 1787.[34]

Friendship: In an open letter to Horatio Townsend and Tim Deasy and the inhabitants of Courtmacsherry Bay in 1789, Patrick Thompson expressed his thanks that, while his vessel *Friendship* lay stranded in their harbour in a very distressed condition, he was not molested in the preservation of ship or cargo.[35]

Hope: Reported lost near Kinsale on 10 December 1790. The master's name was Peters and the vessel was out of Padstow bound for Cork.[36]

Saltan or *Susan*: Reported stranded near Kinsale on 11 November 1791. This vessel was on a voyage from Charleston (USA) to Liverpool. The captain's name was Hardy and the ship was a total loss.[37]

Daniel & Harriot: Reported lost near Kinsale on 27 January 1792. She was out of Limerick and all hands were lost.[38]

Mary: Reported lost near Kinsale on 28 November 1794. The vessel was on a voyage from Bideford to Cork and was lost in a violent gale. The master's name was Nicolls and all the crew were saved.[39]

Nancy: Reported lost at the Old Head on 30 December 1794. This 48-ton vessel out of Poole was on a voyage from Swansea to Cork and the master's name was Collins.[40]

Hope: Reported lost offshore from Kinsale on 27 January 1795.

'Master Custance, from Alicant to Dublin, is taken by privateers off Kinsale Bay, and sunk'.[41]

33   Jerome Lordan.*The Coastal Placenames of Courcey's,* unpublished thesis, Boole Library, UCC, 2012.
34   C. O'Mahony & T.Cadogan, 'Shipwrecks of the Co Cork Coast up to 1810'. p 28.
35   Ibid, p.21.
36   B.T. & R. Larn. *Shipwreck Index of the Irish Coast.*
37   Ibid.
38   Ibid.
39   Ibid.
40   Ibid.
41   Ibid.

Trompeuse: A brig-sloop man o'war captured from the French on 12 January 1794 by the *Sphinx* off Cape Clear. This vessel was taken into Royal Naval service and her armament increased from 16 to 18 guns. On 15 July 1796, she was off Kinsale and sent a boat ashore to bring off fresh vegetables and supplies, the ship closing the land in the afternoon in order to recover the boat. She entered Kinsale roads and, off Crohoge Point, miss-stayed and was forced to anchor, but the incoming tide and southerly wind forced her onto the Farmer Rock. Various dockyard vessels and craft came out to assist. The ship was lightened by taking out her guns, ammunition and stores and every effort was made to get her afloat. Unfortunately, on the ebb tide several of her hull planks gave way as she settled on the rock and commenced to fill. By 2am, she was completely flooded and the crew were ordered to abandon ship using various boats and rafts, the man o' war being deserted by 9 am. Dockyard craft partially dismantled her hull for the timber as best they could, but the lower part of the hull was abandoned.[42]

George: Lost near Kinsale Harbour on 2 February 1796. This ship was en route from Newcastle to Carthagena under Master White when she went ashore.[43]

Unidentified vessel: Reported to be on the shore at the Old Head on 31 January 1797. The vessel, a galliott, was on a voyage from Oporto to Liverpool.[44]

Mary Christina: Reported lost near Kinsale on 7 February 1797. The vessel was on a voyage from Lisbon to Liverpool and the master's name was Lioevils.[45]

Emerald or Emerald Isle: Believed to have foundered about 11 miles west of Kinsale in 1798. The American ship from Galveston in Texas is believed to have been carrying supplies for the 1798 insurgents from America. A story tells that of casks of coins were among the cargo landed at Garretstown.[46]

Elizabeth: Reported lost on the shore near the Old Head on 10 October 1797. The ship was on a voyage from Bremen to Cork and the master's name was Volmers.[47]
Boyd: Reported stranded near the Old Head on 30 November 1798. This 163 ton brigantine was en route from Bristol to Cork. The crew were saved and the master was named Leighton.[48]

Dispatch: Reported on the shore near Kinsale on 30 November 1798. This vessel was bound for Cork from Barnstable and the master's name was Squire.[49]

Alligator: Reported on the shore near Kinsale on 5 March 1799. This 270- ton American ship was making a passage from Portsmouth (USA) to Cork and her master's name was Harris.[50]

42   Ibid.
43   *Historic Shipwrecks of the East & West Cork Coast.*
44   B.T. & R. Larn. *Shipwreck Index of Ireland.*
45   Ibid.
46   E.J. Bourke, vol 1, p.119.
47   B.T. & R. Larn, *Shipwreck Index of the Irish Coast.*
48   Ibid.
49   Ibid.
50   Ibid.

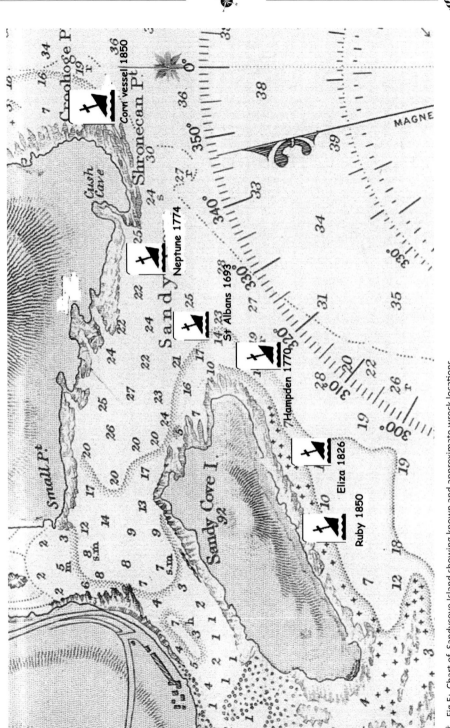

Fig.5: Chart of Sandycove Island showing known and approximate wreck locations.

Chapter II: 1800-1850

Mona: Reported on the shore at Kinsale Harbour on 31 January 1800.
This fully-rigged ship of 176 tons was armed with seven six-pounder guns and seven four-pounder carriage guns. The vessel was on a voyage from Surinam to Liverpool and the master's name was Maudry.[51]

Gravalia: Reported lost off Kinsale on 30 December 1800.
This ship was sailing from Spain to Hamburg and the crew were saved. The master's name was Icelerbom.[52]

Betsy: Reported totally lost near the Old Head on 11 January 1803. The vessel was on a voyage from Swansea to Cork. The captain's name was Fry and the crew were saved.[53]

Penquin: Lost offshore from Kinsale on 17 January 1803. The master's name was Peele of Appledore and the ship was carrying a cargo of coal.[54]

Aspinal: Driven ashore after striking wreckage on 1 February 1803. The vessel was on a voyage from Cork to Barbados and the skipper's name was McCarthy.[55]

Dart: This sailing vessel was lost in Broadstrand Bay on 15 September1804. The master's name was Anderson and the ship was on a voyage from Belfast to Gibraltar. The crew were saved.[56]

Neptune: Wrecked in Courtmacsherry Bay on 4 November 1804. The vessel was bound for Cork with a cargo of coal under Captain John Wilson and the crew were saved.[57]

Unidentified vessel: Reported on the shore near Kinsale on 1 January 1805. The vessel, a sloop was on a voyage from Wales to Cork with a cargo of coal.[58]

Hasodlass: Reported as a total loss near Kinsale on 8 January 1805.The vessel was commanded by Humphreys and was on a voyage from Caernarfon to London.[59]

Betsey: Stranded in Courtmacsherry Bay on 19 September 1805. This vessel was on a voyage from St Thomas to Liverpool.[60]

Peggy: Lost in Courtmacsherry Bay on 22 October 1805. She was originally the 45.5 ton French schooner St Pierre and was taken as a prize by the British.[61]

---

51   B.T. & R. Larn, *Shipwreck Index of Ireland.* Vol 6, Section 4.
52   Ibid.
53   Ibid.
54   Ibid.
55   Ibid.
56   Ibid.
57   Ibid.
58   Ibid.
59   Ibid.
60   Ibid.
61   Ibid.

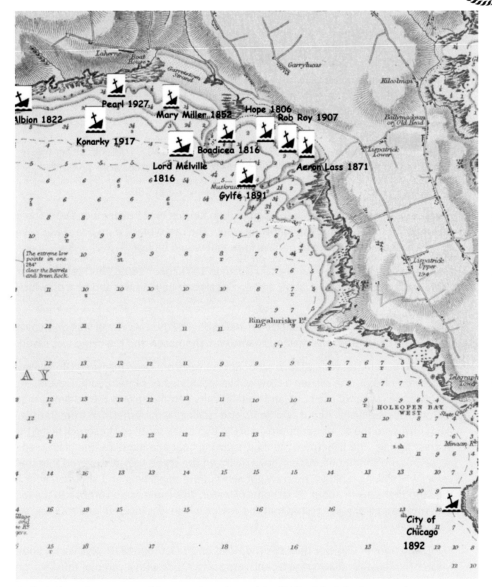

⚓ Fig.6: Chart of eastern part of Courtmacsherry Bay and the Old Head depicting known and approximate locations of wrecks.

Hope: Reported wrecked near the Old Head on 18 February 1806. The vessel was on a voyage from Jamaica to Liverpool, under Captain McEwing. One man was drowned.[62]

62   Ibid.

The other report for the *Hope* comes from a different source. The same vessel was driven ashore on the strand to the west of the Old Head on 6 February 1806 (date differs from Larn source) and totally wrecked. Her multinational crew of 14 clung to the wreck from which they were rescued by the local people at great risk, with the loss of only one life. Among the crew was the captain-owner of a ship in the West India trade who had lost his ship off Jamaica and in this wreck had lost the few pounds he had salvaged from his misfortune. The Kearneys of Garretstown gave aid and succour to the victims.[63]

Union: Reported lost near Barry's Point on 23 October 1807. This ship under master Bigley and laden with staves was driven on shore and the crew were saved.[64]

Annabella: Reported wrecked in Kinsale on 10 November 1807.[65]

Rising Sun: Driven ashore on her beam ends in Kinsale on 27 December 1807. She got off without much damage the following week. The cargo of wine on board was saved, but it was feared the cargo of barilla (soda ash) would be lost.[66]

Unidentified galliot: Lost near the Old Head on 13 October 1809. This French vessel was captured by a Guernsey privateer and had a cargo of balk timber and boards, which were saved.[67]

Louisa: Stranded at Courtmacsherry on 24 October 1809. This vessel was on a voyage from Malta to London. The master's name was Thompson and the cargo was saved.[68]

Yellow Branch: In the year 1810, a schooner set sail from Courtmacsherry for Newport for a cargo of coal. She carried a crew of five including her captain, John Travers. He was also the owner of the boat and had difficulty getting crew as they claimed that she was unseaworthy. About two hours after sailing, some fishermen from Barry's Point observed the schooner approximately two miles south of Horserock flying the distress signals. The fishermen manned a rowing boat and made for the distressed vessel in calm conditions. When they arrived on the scene they discovered that the vessel was sinking rapidly. The crew got away in the ship's boat and about an hour later the schooner sank in about 20 fathoms of water. This came as no surprise to the local fishermen and it was suggested that the vessel, which was insured for £300, was sunk deliberately.[69]

Fly: This schooner was lost near the Old Head on 22 October 1810. This vessel under Master Harker was on a voyage from Liverpool to Africa with a cargo of muskets, only a small part of which were saved.[70] It was reported that most of the 100 stands of arms

63   C.O' Mahony & T.Cadogan,'Shipwrecks on the Cork Coast up to 1810' in Harbour Lights No 1. *Journal of The Great Island Historical Society,* 1988, p.22.
64   B.T & R. Larn, *Shipwreck Index of the Irish Coast.*
65   Ibid.
66   www.corkshipwrecks.net
67   B.T & R. Larn, *Shipwreck Index of the Irish Coast.*
68   Ibid.
69   *Irish Folklore Commission,* Schools Collection, Kilbrittain 1939. (Written by Patrick Keohane, Barleyfield and told to him by James Keohane of the same address).
70   B.T.& R.Larn. *Shipwreck Index of Ireland.*

she carried were salvaged by the natives. James Crofts, a local gentleman, was credited with saving the residue of the guns and powder barrels that comprised the cargo.[71]

Caroline: This sloop went ashore in Bullen's Bay on 16 November 1812. The master of the vessel was James Mullins, the crew were all saved and the cargo unloaded and saved. The vessel came off the following month.[72]

Worsly: Totally lost near Kinsale Harbour on 8 December 1812. This vessel carrying a cargo of coal was out of Workington and bound for Kinsale. All the crew were saved.[73]

Pearl: Totally wrecked near the Old Head on 22 December 1814. This London vessel was on a voyage from Malaga to Dublin under the command of Captain Callow. A small part of the cargo was saved.[74] Another ship of the same name was lost at Garretstown in 1927.

Elizabeth: Was wrecked on Courtmacsherry Bar on 22 December 1814. This vessel under Captain Williams was out of Burry Port, Carmarthenshire, for Cork.[75]

Lord Melville and *Boadicea:*

On 25 January 1816, three troop transport ships, the *Lord Melville*, the *Boadicea* and the *Seahorse* left Ramsgate in the south of England to undertake a voyage to Cork. These three vessels carried a total of 1,070 passengers. These consisted mainly of troops who were returning from the peninsula war, with women, children and crew making up the lesser numbers. On 29 January, the vessels rounded Land's End as the weather freshened from the south-south-east. The weather further freshened to a full gale, and the *Seahorse* took a course for Waterford, whilst the other troop carriers took a more westerly course for Cork. The *Seahorse* met its fate off Tramore strand where all but thirty of the troop of 394 were lost.

> Further to the west on the evening of the 30th the other two vessels were observed from the shore as they struggled with the weather after overshooting Cork harbour. They were now in a precarious position with the shoals of Courtmacsherry bay ahead of them as they ran before the weather. Word had filtered through to the authorities in Kinsale and the Limerick Militia under the directions of Mr Pratt, the port surveyor took the ferry across to the western side of the harbour at the Dock from Kinsale. When they arrived there they found that one of the ships (*Lord Melville*) had been driven ashore among the rocks - that shortly after she struck, her boat had been launched and smashed with five men- two that were officers and their wives, an assistant surgeon, a sergeant, his wife and child had got in to the boat in the hope of making the shore. She was struck by a wave and swamped before making the shore, all perished with the exception of one seaman.[76]
> The other victims remained on the ship, there was nothing they could do only wait for the falling tide and hope that the brig would hold together. Low water was around midnight. With the help of Lieutenant Harty a long spar was lashed from the nearest dry rock to the vessels bow. The intention was to pass everyone on board along this spar. At 11pm, this was carried out with everyone getting off safely.[77]

71   C. O'Mahony & T.Cadogan, 'Shipwrecks of the Cork Coast' in Harbour Lights No 1, p. 21.
72   www.corkshipwrecks.net
73   B.T & R. Larn, *Shipwreck Index of the Irish Coast*.
74   Ibid.
75   Ibid.
76   *Cork Mercantile Chronicle*. 2 February 1816.
77   Raymond White.*Their Bones are Scattered*: A History of the Old Head of Kinsale and Surrounding Area. Kilmore Enterprises. 2003. p. 109.

Lieutenant Harty, with equal promptitude, had arranged for their being distributed among the neighbouring cabins, and they were marched off according, to return early next morning for the purpose of endeavouring to get out the arms and accoutrements. Nothing, however, could possibly be done towards that end by the early return of the tide and consequent impossibility of access to the ship. The few men and officers who were enabled to return on board reported to me the almost total destruction of all the baggage from the sea it was swimming in, and the pillaging that took place after the troops were got on shore. Finding the men much in need of repose, and the day advancing, I directed their proceeding to Kinsale, leaving two officers parties from the 59th and 62nd Regiments to remain in protection of the ship, conjointly with a party from the Limerick Militia.[78]

⚓ Fig 7: The Lord Melville & the Boadicea were lost in the approximate positions illustrated by red stars on the *Curlán* between the White Strand and Garretstown Strand /*Tráigh a' Lahern* in 1816. *Courtesy of Kevin Dwyer.*

The *Boadicea* had dropped her anchor and stood off from the shore as the *Lord Melville* broke up and the passengers got off at low water. In many cases the wind will pick up with the flood tide and this, possibly, was one of the contributing factors that further jeopardised the safety of that vessel.

At the commencement of the night the brig *"Boadicea"* being at anchor and further off the shore, had to all appearances much greater chance of escape than the ship. She was distinctly seen by the revenue officers and military party with a light at her topmast till after midnight. The light and the vessel then disappeared altogether. It still blew a tremendous gale of wind right on the shore; the sea ran mountains high; the rain poured down in torrents, and the night was pitch dark. When the morning dawned the gloomy apprehension of the party from Kinsale seemed but too well founded, as the brig had disappeared. However, after a diligent search for some time along the shore, her fragments

78   Robert Day. Wreck of the Transport "Lord Melville" in *Journal of the Cork Historical and Archaeological Society,* Vol.8, Second Series, (1902), p. 55.

were discerned among the rocks between the two strands of Garretstown, where she had been driven after parting from her anchors in the night. Upon approaching the wreck a most heartrending scene of misery, desolation, and death presented itself. The vessel seemed to be a confused mass of timber, planks and boards, broken to pieces and intermixed with piles of dead bodies, men, women and children.[79]

The vessel broke up very fast and upwards of 80 people clung to an elevated rock outcrop known as the *Curlán* which separates the two strands of Garretstown (*Tráigh a' Lahern*) and Garrylucas (White Strand). The recovery party, which included the Sea Fencibles, a naval militia established during the Napoleonic War, the Limerick Militia and a large number of local people tried to convey to the rock-bound survivors to stay where they were until near low water when the elevated rock became accessible from the main body of land. The elevated part of the *Curlán* is approximately 300 yards from the mainland and is surrounded by water for about three hours before high water and three hours after. In spite of the pleas from the rescuing party that they should remain where they were, about thirty tried in vain to make for the shore and most perished attempting to do so. The rest of the fifty or so survivors stayed put until low tide, allowing them to depart their watery fortress by clambering across the rocks.

A plaque on the wall of St Multose Church, Kinsale, commemorates the officers and troops who perished on the *Boadicea*. In 1900, a Mr Robert Day was walking across the shore near the site of the two shipwrecks when he came along a mound of sand ten feet high and forty feet long. The mound was located near the present car park; this area consisted of sand dunes prior to the construction of the parking area today. The human remains were clearly to be seen, and he recalled being told of local people finding buttons bearing the number "82". He contacted the regiment with a proposal to move the mortal remains to Old Court graveyard. The memorial to the victims was restored by Raymond White and Philip McCarthy in the recent past and can now be viewed at this long disused burial ground.

Flora: Driven on the shore near the Old Head on 9 January 1818. This ship was out of Québec for London under Master Caldwell and the cargo was expected to be saved.[80]

Caledonia: Driven on the shore near the Old Head on 12 January 1818. This vessel was out of Prince Edward Island, bound for Cork, under the command of Captain Stewart. The crew and cargo were saved.[81]

---

79   Robert Day. The Wreck of the Transport *"Boadicea"* in *Journal of the Cork Historical and Archaeological Society*, Vol 7, Second Series, (1901), p. 132.
80   B.T. & R. Larn. *Shipwreck Index of Ireland.*
81   Ibid.

Sylvan: 11 November 1818

The *Sylvan* was wrecked when it was wedged into the channel that separates the Great Sovereign Island into two parts. This occurred about 12 noon in a heavy sea and foggy conditions. Later that day, when the fog dissipated, it was evident from the shore that something was amiss in the channel. After she broke up, a boy was seen clinging to the rigging and an attempt was made to rescue him. However due to the conditions and closing darkness this was not possible. It was a very windy night with heavy rain. At first light the boatmen of Oysterhaven rowed out to the island in the heaving sea. As they proceeded they came upon much wreckage. They also saw the boy clinging precariously to the swaying mast and, given the weather conditions could do nothing to rescue him. These circumstances were communicated to Mr Newman, the Sovereign of Kinsale (the sovereign fulfilled the role of mayor). He proceeded to the scene and offered a reward of ten guineas to the crew of a Kinsale boat if they could rescue the boy. At this stage the boy was on the island and many people had gathered on the cliffs to view the situation. The weather was relentless and the boat crews of two Oysterhaven vessels and one from Kinsale could not get close to the island for several hours. One effort was made to land on the island by a boat from Oysterhaven with a small punt in tow. On coming as close as the sea allowed them, three men took to the punt and were almost immediately put up on the shore of the island by the swell, at the spot where the boy stood. They threw him a rope and at the same moment an incoming wave took the punt away, partially filling up and all but throwing the rescuers into the water. The punt and crew were hauled back aboard the standby vessel and the crew made gestures to the boy to tie the rope around his middle and they would pull him. However the lad ignorant of their gestures or too afraid, threw the rope back. As they retreated to land for the night they saw the boy consume wild plants, which the island abounded in, before the fog once again concealed him from their observation. The following day the weather was as bad as the previous days and the various crews knew that another night would probably be fatal for the victim. On board one of the Oysterhaven boats, the owner, a man by the name of Jack Carty, allowed a rope to be tied around him and plunged into the water in an attempt to reach the boy. He succeeded in getting ashore and clambered up the cliff face to fix his own rope around the poor boy who was now in a weakened state. The lad was placed on the same point that Carty landed on and pushed into the water where the boatmen rapidly retrieved him to the vessel. A rope was then thrown to Carty who did the same, and he too was pulled aboard his own boat. This account was given in Tuckey's *'Cork Remembrancer'* and *JCHAS* (Antiquarian Remains in Kinsale District). Little detail of the wreck itself was given.

According to www.coastguardsofyesteryear.org/articles, Jack Carty was afterwards known as 'Jack of the rock'. He was a native of Pallice, near Oysterhaven, a fisherman and boat owner, he had also spent some time in the merchant service. He was described by those who remember him as a man of fine physique and he was buried in Kilmonogue graveyard near Mountlong Castle, a short distance from Oysterhaven. The boy survived and settled in the area.

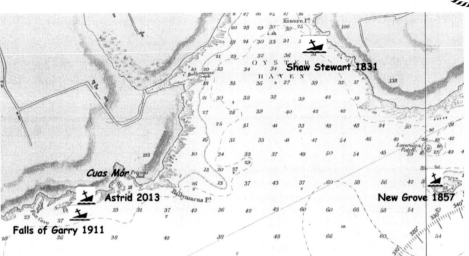

⚓ Fig.8: Chart of Sovereign Islands and Oysterhaven illustrating known wreck sites.

Sally: Reported lost off Kinsale on 23 February 1819. Out of Newbury Port, bound for Liverpool, crew saved.[82]

Venus: Lost on the shore near the Old Head on 16 October 1820. The master was named Le Feurre from Newfoundland, crew (except the carpenter) were saved.[83]

Resolution: Totally wrecked near Kinsale on 15 December 1820. This London vessel under master Blaney was on a voyage from Newfoundland to Liverpool and the crew were saved by boats from the shore with much difficulty.[84]

Shamrock: Wrecked coming out of Kinsale Harbour on 17 November 1821. The master of the vessel named Colman was out of Kinsale and bound for Limerick. Part of the cargo was saved.[85]

82   Ibid.
83   Ibid.
84   Ibid.
85   Ibid.

The wreck of the *Albion* in Courtmacsherry Bay 1822.

The following is part of a nineteenth-century account from *The Mariner's Chronicle* of events surrounding the wreck of the *Albion*, west of Garretstown Strand, in April 1822.

Few instances have occurred of a shipwreck more distressing in its circumstances, and more calamitous in its destruction of valuable lives and property, than that of the *Albion*. It will long be remembered, even in history, from the melancholy fate of two distinguished men among its passengers, Lefebvre-Desnouettes, one of Napoleon's generals, and Professor Fisher, of Yale College who, though young in age, had already accomplished much in science, and gave large promise of future eminence. The following statements, published at the time in the Liverpool papers, will furnish the reader a full account of the sad event. This fine ship sailed from New-York on the 1st of April 1822, with a crew of 24 men and about 28 passengers. On the 22nd she was entirely lost on the coast of Ireland, near the Old Head of Kinsale. Only two of the passengers and seven of the crew were saved. All the particulars of this melancholy shipwreck which we have received in town up to the hour that we are writing, (April 27th) are contained in two letters published in the Mercury yesterday, and which we give beneath; the one from Jacob Mark, US consul at Kinsale, to Messrs. Cropper, Benson, and Co. Liverpool, the other from an eye witness of the scene, a Mr Purcell, agent of the gentleman to whom this is addressed and which has been forwarded here by the gentleman, for the information of those interested.

Kinsale, April 22, 1822.

On my arrival at this place early this morning, I was informed of the melancholy fate of the ship *Albion*, Captain Williams, one of the line of packet ships from New –York to your port; she was cast away before daylight this morning, to the westward of the Old Head, near a place called Garretstown, and I grieve to say, poor Captain Williams is no more. There were 22 passengers aboard in the cabin, 15 men and 7 women, all of whom have met a watery grave, with the exception of a young man from Boston, I understand; and he is so exhausted, he could not give the names of the others, or any particulars; seven of the crew are saved, one of the mates and six men. I am informed that there was a considerable sum in specie on board; part of the deck only floated ashore. Last night was very tempestuous ; and it seems the ship lost her masts about ten o'clock, carrying a press of sail off the land, wind S.S.E. which was the cause of the misfortune ; it was about three o'clock this morning that she struck a ledge of rocks, and went to pieces. I understand a few bales of cotton have come ashore. It is my intention to go to the spot and render any service in my power to the unfortunate survivors: and if anything particular comes to my knowledge relative to this truly awful and melancholic catastrophe, I shall drop you a line, in haste your sincere friend.

Jacob Mark.

To Messrs. Cropper, Benson & Co

Garretstown, April 22, 1822.   Honoured Sir,-At some time before 4 o'clock this morning I was informed that a ship was cast on the rocks at the bottom of your dairy farms, to which place I immediately repaired; and at about the centre of the two farms found a vessel on the rocks, under a very high cliff. At this time, as it blew a dreadful gale, with a spring tide and approaching high water, the sea ran mountains high; however, I descended with some men as far down the cliff as the dashing of the waves would permit us to go with safety, and there we had the horrid spectacle of viewing five dead bodies stretched on the deck, and four other fellow creatures distractedly calling for assistance, which we were unable to afford them, as certain death would have attended the attempt to render them any. Of those in this perilous situation, one was a female, whom, though it was impossible, from the roaring of the sea, to hear her, yet, from her gestures and stretching of her hands, we judged to be calling and imploring for our assistance. At this time the greater part of the vessel lay on the rock, and part of her stern, where this poor woman lay, projected over a narrow creek that divides this rock from another. Here the sea ran over her with the greatest fury, yet she kept a firm hold, which it much astonished me she could do; but we soon perceived that the vessel was broke across where she projected over the rock, and after many waves dashing against her, this part of the vessel rolled into the waves, and we had the heart rendering scene of seeing the woman perish. Three men lay toward the stern of the vessel, one of whom stuck to a mast which projected toward the cliff, to which, after many attempts, we succeeded in throwing a rope, and brought him safe ashore. Another we also saved; but the constant dashing of the waves put an end to the sufferings of the others. This vessel proves to be the *Albion*, of New-York, packet Captain Williams, which place she left on the 1st instance for Liverpool, with a cargo of cotton, raw turpentine, rice, and with about 28 passengers. Her crew consisted of 24, and of the whole there have been saved only nine, making the sufferers amount to 43. Out of the passengers there have been saved two. The bodies of five men and two women have been picked up. After doing everything possible for these poor creatures, I exerted myself with Mr. Gibbons in saving the private property of the poor sailors and passengers, and succeeded in saving some of their trunks. I have brought four of these poor creatures here. Mr. Gibbons has taken three, and two more remain at the dairy-men's houses; from whence they were too weak to be removed. Captain Williams is among the sufferers. As I know your feelings towards those thus situated, I have taken the liberty of preparing some thin boards to make coffins for these seven. She is now completely gone to pieces. She was, I think, as fine a vessel of her description as could be seen. My situation does not allow me to say more at present, as I was never more fatigued, and remain,

> Honoured Sir,
> Your ever-grateful and obedient servant,
> (Signed)   John Purcell

> *To Thomas Rochford, Esq.*
> *Kinsale*, April 26, 1822   On my arrival here on

the 22nd I wrote you a hasty letter, apprising you of the melancholy fate of the ship. I went over the fatal spot, and I cannot describe the scene that presented itself to my view, nor am I disposed to dwell on the heart-rending scene. I shall be as brief as possible.   Henry Cammyer, the first mate, is saved, and six of the crew. The whole company on board, including passengers amounted to fifty-six, of whom forty-five perished, and nine are saved. The log-book being lost, the mate could not give me a list of the passengers; but, from memory, he has given me the names of eighteen, which are annexed. As the bodies that were found lay on the shore, the mate pointed out to me their respective names, which were put on paper and placed on each body, and I gave directions that the graves should be numbered, and a list made out, which I expected to get this day, by which it can be easily ascertained where each body lies in the grave-yard. A clergyman attended the melancholy procession. This may be of some consolation to the afflicted relatives of the dead. Very little of the wreck remains, and the country people are carrying it off in all directions, in small pieces. I have desired the remnants to be put up at auction and sold. I enquired of the mate about the specie; there were two boxes for you, two for Professor Fisher, a passenger, beside a packet of dollars belonging to the only cabin passenger saved, Mr Everhart, of Pennsylvania, who is very ill in bed. The mate thought I had not the least chance of recovering a dollar. I however thought otherwise. I accordingly took aside a confidential man, John Purcell, who is in the employment, and enjoys the unlimited confidence of my worthy and respectable friend, Thomas Rochford, ESQ, of Garretstown, who owns all the land in the neighbourhood. I told him to employ a few men, on whose honesty I could depend, and set them to work to examine the spot where I received the mate's report the money might be, and that I would give him a good commission (I think I said five per cent.) if he could prevent plunder, and save the property. Late last night I received the in-closed by express, and am now on the point of returning to the wreck. The box was broken and plunder attempted.

> Yours truly,   Jacob Mark
> *Cropper, Benson & Co*

> *Garretstown, Thursday evening. April 25, 1822*

Sir- I have only time to inform you that we found, near where the wreck of the *Albion* lay, this day, different gold coins in a small box, in all, by a rough calculation, amounting to upward of 3000 in number.. The coins being many of them foreign, and of different sizes, prevents me from being able to ascertain the exact sum, but it has all been brought up here safe, and counted in the presence of Mr Pratt, the officer of the customs, Mr Lemon and myself. I hasten to acquaint you of this pleasing circumstance. I have the honour to be, sir, your most obedient and humble servant,

John Purcell *to Jacob Mark, Esq.*

From the Southern Reporter of Saturday

The *Albion*, whose loss at Garretstown Bay we first mentioned in our paper of Tuesday, was one of the first class of ships between Liverpool and New-York, and was 500 tons burthen. We have since learned some further particulars, by which it appears that her loss was attended with circumstances of a peculiarly afflicting nature. She had lived out the tremendous gale of the entire day on Sunday, and Captain Williams consoled his passengers, at 8 o'clock in the evening, with the hope of being able to reach Liverpool on the day but one after, which cheering expectation induced, most of the passengers, particularly the females, to retire to rest. In some short time, however, a violent squall came on, which in a moment carried away the masts and there being no possibility of disengaging them from the rigging, they so encumbered the hull that she became unmanageable, and drifted at the mercy of the waves, till the lighthouse at the Old Head was discovered, the wreck still nearing in, when the captain told the sad news to the passengers that there was no longer any hope and soon after she struck. From thenceforward all was distress and confusion. The vessel soon went to pieces, and of the crew and passengers, only six of the former, and one of the latter were saved. The mate is among the preserved, and that preservation was almost miraculous. He was thrown on the cliff by a wave, and succeeded in climbing to the top of it, when another took him off. He was thus thrown back again, and was more fortunate; but his appearance bespeaks the sufferings he endured from the beating of his body against the rocks. He is dreadfully bruised. The number of passengers, we believe, is twenty-five. Of these, as we have already stated, only one was saved, a gentleman of Boston, who traded with Liverpool. He had arrived at New-York almost as the *Albion* was on the point of sailing, and had not time to get bills for a large sum of specie which he had. It was therefore shipped and lost. Several of the bodies have been washed ashore, and Jacob Mark, Esq, the American Consul at this port, having repaired to the scene where the wreck took place, immediately on learning the melancholy intelligence, had done everything befitting his situation and a man of humanity, under these circumstances. He has provided coffins for the bodies, and caused them to be interred with their respective names affixed, having first had the mate to point them out, in order that if the families of them should wish hereafter to have the bodies removed, they may be enabled to do so.

It appears from a comparison of the several accounts which have been published of the loss of the *Albion*, that for the first twenty days after leaving New York, the weather was moderate and favourable; and that about one o'clock on Sunday 21, the ship made the south of Ireland. Soon after a gale commenced, which blew the remainder of the day with great violence. About half past eight in the evening the *Albion* shipped a heavy sea, which threw her on her beam ends, and took the mainmast by the deck, the head of the mizenmast, and fore topmast, and swept the decks clear of everything, including boats, compasses, & co, and stove in all the hatches, state-rooms, and bulwarks in the cabin, which was nearly filled with water. At the same time six of the crew, and one cabin passenger, Mr Cosgrove of New York were swept overboard. The axes being lost, no means remained of clearing the deck, and the ship was unmanageable. About three o'clock the ship struck a reef of rocks, about one hundred yards from the main land. This as afterward appeared was in Courtmacsherry Bay, about three miles from the Old Head of Kinsale. In about half an hour the ship went to pieces; and all the cabin passengers apart from Mr. W. Everhart of Chester, Pennsylvania, were lost. It is understood that Professor Fisher, as well as some others, was considerably injured when the masts were carried away; and at the time the other passengers went on deck, after the captain had informed them of their imminent danger, he remained below in his berth. Whether he afterward came up, and what were the particular circumstances of his death are unknown.[86]

---

86   *The Mariner's Chronicle:* Containing narratives of the most remarkable disasters at sea, such as shipwrecks, storms, fires, and famines, also naval engagements, piratical adventures, incidents of discovery, and other extraordinary and interesting occurrences. New Haven: G.W.Gorton, 1835.

↥ Fig. 9: The *Albion* was lost here a short distance west of the Devil's Eye, marked by a red star in 1822. The spot is since known as *Cuas Albion*. The *Pearl* was lost a short distance to the right extreme and off the image in 1927, with a loss of all hands. *Courtesy of Kevin Dwyer.*

Thomas & Ann: Reported lost in the west part of Kinsale Harbour on 7 November 1823. This vessel from Kinsale was lost with two of its crew.[87]

Eliza: This brigantine was lost on Sandycove Island on 15 January 1826. This ship of 147 tons from Cardigan under Master Davis was totally wrecked and all the crew except one were rescued by the preventive boat under Lieutenant Barry.[88]

Heart of Oak: Lost on 15 February 1827. This brigantine of 120 tons from Maryport and laden with coal, was lost at the east side of the Old Head in a snowstorm from the east-south-east. All her crew were lost.[89]

Shaw Stewart: Was wrecked near Oysterhaven on 26 November 1831. Her master was Sinclair. The voyage was from Greenock to Limerick.[90]

Friends of Chepstow: Reported lost at North Bank, Kinsale on an unknown date in 1833. The vessel was en route from Newport to Liverpool. Captain Townley of the *Thetis,* while returning from Dublin, rescued some of the crew off Kinsale.[91] The whereabouts of the North Bank are not known today. A possibility for this location

87   B.T. & R. Larn. *Shipwreck Index of Ireland.*
88   Ibid.
89   *www.Irishshipwrecks.com*
90   E.J. Bourke. *Shipwrecks of the Irish Coast 1582-2000, Vol 3.*
91   *Historic Shipwrecks of the East & West Cork Coast, Dúchas:* The Heritage Service, 2000.

is the most northern part of the Labadie Bank, about 53 miles south-south-east of the Bulman Buoy. This is a well-known fishing area to British, Irish and French fishermen. It is a place to be avoided in bad weather, due to the shallow nature of the bank.

Mary: Lost at the Barrel Rocks on 1 May 1833. Vessel was en route from Demerera to Dublin under Master Morris.[92]

Try Again: Stranded near Kinsale, total loss, on 24 November 1835. This vessel was out of Quebec, for Cork.[93]

Bacchus: Lost at Kinsale on 24 November 1835. The vessel was en route from Bathurst to Bideford.[94]

John Vianna: This vessel out of Palermo for Liverpool, was lost on the Barrel Rocks with all hands on board 30 December 1835.[95]

Spanish brigantine: Wrecked at the Old Head on 20 January 1836.[96]

Repartere: A French brigantine was washed ashore in a gale from the east-south-east at Dooneen on 20 January 1838. The crew were all saved and the cargo recovered.[97] The ship was carrying a cargo of brandy and the crew walked ashore and went into a thatched public house close by. This was the first intimation that a ship had come ashore. About a week later, a second gale, more fearsome than the first, completely smashed the vessel. Various efforts were made by country people to secure possession of the kegs of Brandy. The military guards and coastguards raided the locality and smashed any salvaged kegs to save drinkers from over indulgence.[98]

92   T. Cadogan. *Mizen Historical Journal.*
93   B.T & R. Larn, *Shipwreck Index of the Irish Coast.*
94   E.J. Bourke. *Shipwrecks of the Irish Coast, 1105-1993, Vol 1.*
95   *Historic Shipwrecks of the East & West Cork Coast.*
96   E.J. Bourke. *Shipwrecks of the Irish Coast, 1582-2000, Vol 3.*
97   www.corkshipwrecks.net
98   *Breathnacht Papers.* PR 24(27) Box 4 (8).

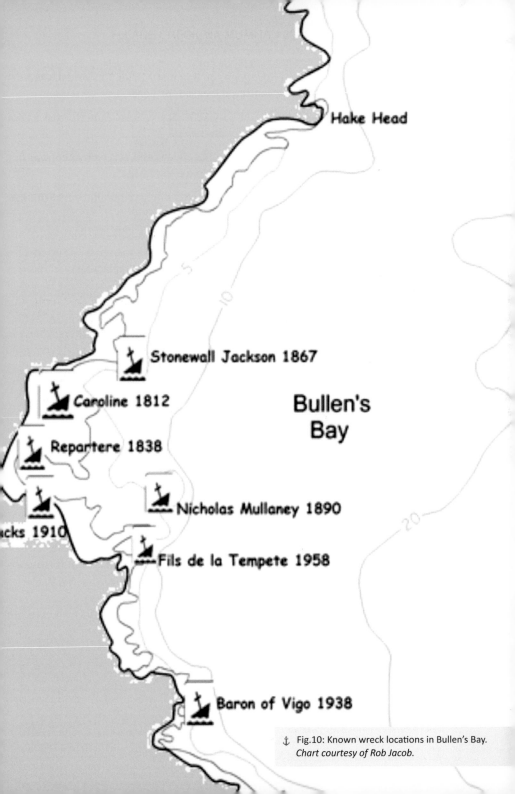

Hake Head

Stonewall Jackson 1867

Caroline 1812

Bullen's
Bay

Repartere 1838

Nicholas Mullaney 1890

cks 1910

Fils de la Tempete 1958

Baron of Vigo 1938

⚓ Fig.10: Known wreck locations in Bullen's Bay.
Chart courtesy of Rob Jacob.

Unknown sloop: Wrecked near the Sovereigns on 2 January 1838. This vessel was laden with herrings and was caught in a gale from the east-south-east.[99]

Mary: Wrecked at the Old Head on 14 February 1839. She was en route from Liverpool to Limerick under Captain Fudge. All hands were saved.[100]

Warrior: Stranded at Coolmain on 18 January 1840. This vessel was en route from Liverpool to Charlestown and is expected to become a total wreck.[101]

Friends of Liberty: A local schooner out of Kinsale was homeward bound when she was lost near Kinsale on 15 March 1841.[102]

Latona: Went ashore between Kinsale and Courtmacsherry, 7 February 1842. The vessel was wrecked and had come from Alexandria under a captain named Sutton.[103] The Dublin Custom house records state that she was lost in Courtmacsherry Harbour.

Emma: On 23 January 1843, a Swansea smack stranded near Kinsale. She was en route from Swansea to Kenmare.[104]

Lucy Ann: Was wrecked at Charles Fort on 13 January 1844. She was en route from Ichiboe (South Africa) to Bristol.[105]

Unknown: Wreckage from an unknown ship washed ashore in Kinsale on 18 October 1844.[106]

Dublin: Stranded and wrecked at the Old Head on 20 March 1847. This vessel was carrying a cargo of hides and horns.[107]

Kate: A 67-ton sailing vessel was burnt off Kinsale on 19 April 1847.[108] It seems strange that the next listed vessel has the same name and was lost in the same year. Further research is needed to determine whether they are two different ships.

Kate: Total loss after stranding near Kinsale on 17 December 1847. This vessel was a schooner of 117 tons out of St Ives under Matthews, the ship's master.[109]

Waterloo: Stranded and wrecked inside Kinsale Harbour on 2 March 1848. This schooner of 92 tons was en route from Cork to Bantry.[110] The home port of this vessel was Clonakilty and all of those aboard survived.[111]

99   www.corkshipwrecks.net
100   E.J.Bourke, vol 3.
101   B.T. & R. Larn, *Shipwreck Index of the Irish Coast.*
102   *Historic Shipwrecks of the East & West Cork Coast.*
103   E.J. Bourke, vol 3.
104   *Historic Shipwrecks of the East & West Cork Coast.*
105   Ibid.
106   Ibid.
107   *Cork Examiner,* 25 March 1847.
108   *Historic Shipwrecks of the East & West Cork Coast.*
109   B.T & R. Larn, *Shipwreck Index of the Irish Coast.*
110   Ibid.
111   *Historic Shipwrecks of the East & West Cork Coast. Dúchas:* The Heritage Service, 2000.

A yacht belonging to the Earl of Mountcashel was wrecked on the Bulman Rock, date unknown.[112]

A unidentified smack: Lost on the Horse Rock on 21 October 1848. Crew were saved.[113]

St Amaro: Lost at the Old Head on 4 December 1848. On a voyage from Tercia to Cork.[114]

Duquet: Was driven ashore in Courtmacsherry in a storm and all hands were saved, 15 December 1848.[115] Further details on this event are given in the next page.

Courtmacsherry Bay Shipwrecks on 15 December 1848

The weather leading up to these tragic events all across the northeast Atlantic was very bad, with winds up to hurricane force experienced in some quarters. A litany of shipwrecks is described briefly in press reports stretching from Norway to the Low Countries and out into the western approaches. The winds were coming predominantly from all points between south and west. The following account appeared in the 'Cork Examiner' some days after these fateful events.

Howestrand, December 15th- The *Severn*, barque, for London, from St John's, laden with deals and sleepers, came on shore on the rocky point at the entrance to Howestrand, on Friday morning , and is a total wreck.[116]

Howestrand, December 16th- The barque *Severn,* Master Richard Cresca, has been totally wrecked. The coastguard promptly lent their assistance, and, with the aid of Dennett's rockets, succeeded in putting a line over her by which means the lives of fifteen of the crew were fortunately saved. Two were drowned owing to their own neglect in not securing themselves properly to the hawser. The inhabitants seconded in every way the exertions of the coastguard to render aid. On the previous day Lieutenant Triphook, in the *Hamilton* Revenue Cruiser, proceeded to this vessels assistance. She was reported to be at anchor off the Barrel Rocks. He burned a blue light and fired two rockets, which were answered by the ship's lanterns. The *Hamilton* being steered for the light found her to be the Severn, twenty nine days out, with her masts cut away, and riding easily to her anchor. From the heavy ground sea, and the wind being right in the *Hamilton* could render no assistance further than for Lieutenant Triphook to urge the captain to get his boats ready for landing, but he seemed not inclined to leave the vessel. One boat, with four men, was got out, rowed astern of the cruiser, and the men were pulled up with great difficulty-the boat being set adrift. The gale coming on most heavily, with a tremendous sea, she was unable to remain any longer by the vessel, and having put to sea, by carrying a large press of canvas, she was enabled to be kept off the shore until day light, when she ran for Courtmacsherry harbour, and arrived there safely.[117]

What is remarkable about the fate of the *Severn* is that so many survived given that the wind blew up to hurricane force at the time of the grounding. The coastline here in the inner reaches of the bay is very shoal, with several reefs, the Inner and Outer Barrels, the

---

112   *The Cork Examiner,* 15 December 1848.
113   Ibid.
114   Ibid.
115   *Cork Examiner* , 17 December 1848.
116   *Cork Examiner.* Initial report from the 15 December.
117   *Cork Examiner,* 20 December 1848.

⚓ Fig.11: Howe Strand /*Tráigh an Abha*. The *Severn* was lost here in 1848.   *Courtesy of Kevin Dwyer.*

Blueboy, Brean Rock, the Horse rock, *Carraig a'Broigheall* to name but a few. Howes Strand or *Tráigh an Abha*, as it was known to the native inhabitants, is one of the very few places, given a choice in such circumstances, that grounding would give one a better chance of survival, due to the geography of the coastline. Both the *Albion* and the *Hercules* foundered near here with very few survivors in similar conditions.

Another grounding took place a short distance away to the southwest in Broadstrand/ *Tráigh Claoin* at that time.
A large French brig, of about 300 tons burthen, came on shore about twelve o'clock yesterday, and is now high and dry on the rocks. She is called the *Duchet*, from Bordeaux to Liverpool, with a general cargo of wine, fruit, the greater part of which will be saved should the weather be moderate. The captain's son, who was on board, was drowned in attempting to reach the shore, and the rest of the crew had a narrow escape. We have now four wrecks within a few miles of each other on this coast. It is feared that many vessels foundered at sea during the gale, as the coast is strewn with fragments of wreck.[118]

118 Ibid.

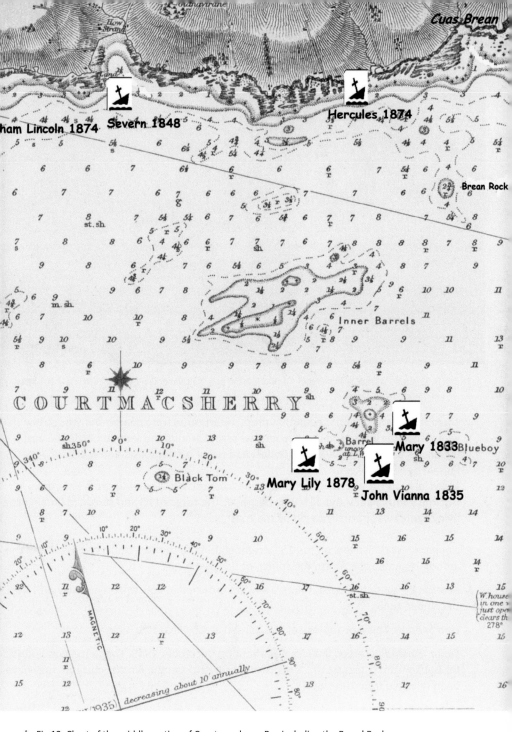

Fig.12: Chart of the middle section of Courtmacsherry Bay including the Barrel Rocks indicating approximate wreck sites.

⚓ Fig.13: Broad Strand/ *Tráigh Claoin.* The *Dart* (1804) and the *Duquet* (1848) were both lost in this bay.
   Courtesy of Kevin Dwyer.

The other wrecks mentioned in that press report came from nearby Dunworley Bay where the *Free Trade* and the *Bayonne* were lost around the same time. To the east in Bullen's Bay, the brig *Albert* of Belfast had to cut off her masts and was towed to Kinsale by two hookers.

In Oysterhaven, a brigantine schooner, the *Nouparell* of Yarmouth, from Palermo, became a total wreck and all hands perished. The cargo of oil and sumac (a tanning and dying agent) was partially saved by the coastguard.[119]

Nouparell: Was also lost on the 15 December 1848 to the east of Kinsale. However, the author is unable to confirm the source of this event.

Bernice: En-route to Genoa, four crew were drowned in Courtmacsherry Bay on 17 December 1848. [120]

Lord Sandon: This 470-ton vessel was burned at Kinsale on 21 February 1849.[121]

Santa Trinidad: wrecked in Kinsale Harbour on December 1849. The vessel was bound for Dublin from Queenstown. The pair of candlesticks in the Kinsale museum may have been salvaged from this ship.[122]

---

119   Ibid.
120   *House of Commons Parliamentary Papers.*
121   Ibid.
122   E.J. Bourke, vol 1, p. 120-21.

⚓ Fig.14: Candlesticks reputed to be from from the Santa Trinidad which was lost in Kinsale Harbour in 1849. These are currently housed in the Kinsale Museum. *Courtesy of Kinsale Museum.*

Ruby: On Saturday night, 29 March 1850 this smack was wrecked at Sandy Cove Island with all hands lost. The circumstances surrounding the disaster are unknown. A headless body was washed ashore at the spot, reported the *Cork Examiner* of Monday 1 April. Part of the wreck floated into Kinsale Harbour. The home port of the vessel was Liverpool.

Corn vessels: Wrecked at the Old Head and Sandy Cove on 30 March 1850. Corn smuggling was prevalent in Kinsale and a mill was constructed at Sandy Cove to store the cargoes. One of these smuggling ships was wrecked on the Old Head when she came too close inshore to avoid two patrol ships. Another vessel also with a similar cargo was lost at Sandy Cove. Part of the wreck floated into Kinsale Harbour.[123] The construction of the Heard Bridge or Western Bridge as it was later known in 1860, about two miles above Kinsale, contributed to the economic decline of Sandycove as a port of discharge. The bridge provided easier access to Courcey country and Sandycove was bypassed.

---

123   Ibid. p.119.

Chapter III: 1851-1877

Austrian brigantine: Lost after contact with another Austrian vessel in Kinsale Harbour, 25 February 1851.[124]

Voyageur: lost at the Old Head on November 1851. The vessel was en route from Galetz to Tralee.[125]

Mary Miller: A 280-ton barque from Cork was returning to her home port from Drogheda in ballast on 29 October 1852 when the master named Hobbs mistook the old lighthouse at the Old Head for Roche's Point. Wind conditions at the time were southeast and up to storm force. On approaching one of the strands on the inside part of the Old Head, he shot his two anchors but drifted onto the shore. The damaged barque was towed off by a steam tug on 5 November and brought to Cork for repairs. The estimate cost of repairs was £1,200, but the ship was only insured for £400.[126]

Andreas: This Hamburg barque was en route from Honduras to Cork with a cargo of mahogany and a crew of ten. She encountered foggy conditions on 1 August 1853 and became stranded on the shore. She sustained some damage and eventually came off. The barque was brought to Queenstown for repairs.[127]

Progress: This eight-year-old steamship of 317 tons, carrying a cargo of grain, was partially wrecked at the Old Head on 9 December 1856. One of the 19 crew on board was lost.[128]

New Grove : This Kinsale smack of 24 tons owned and skippered by John Donovan was en route from Cork to Kinsale, with a crew of three, carrying a cargo of deals when she struck the Little Sovereign on 13 July 1857. She was involved in local coastal trade from Cork to the western ports and never had a chart or a lead-line aboard, nor did she use a pilot, as the master and crew were pilots themselves. When she was off Oysterhaven the main boom and stays were carried away in a southwest gale and the vessel was lost on the aforementioned island.[129]

Genoese Ship: A large American ship the *Western Star* of Boston put into Queenstown (Cobh) on Sunday morning, 30 August 1857. The ship was in a near sinking condition. About 2 am that morning she came into collision with a strange vessel off the Old Head of Kinsale and went right over her sending her to the bottom with all hands aboard. So sudden was the occurrence, the two vessels meeting in the dark, that the crew of the *Western Star* could only make out that the other vessel was a barque, but could not ascertain where she was from. The crewmembers on the deck of the barque appeared

---

124   B.T. & R. Larn, *Shipwreck Index of the Irish Coast*.
125   E.J. Bourke, vol 1, p.121.
126   *Historic Shipwrecks of the East & West Cork Coast, Dúchas*: The Heritage Service, 2000.
127   *Ibid*.
128   Ibid.
129   Ibid.

to be neither American nor British. A Genoese ship also arrived in Queenstown the same day and the captain expressed the view that the vessel was from his own country. However, it could never be established where the vessel was from. The *Western Star* was bound from Rio to Falmouth, for orders, with sugar and rice. She was towed up to Victoria Dock in Passage and it was deduced that several of her planks were started.[130]

John Field: A 25-ton smack registered in Skibbereen and owned by John Field of Whitehall, Skibbereen, was en route from New Ross to her home port via Clonakilty. She was carrying a cargo of coal and was blown off course in a northeast gale when she lost her sails. The two crew members abandoned her when the brigantine *Eugenie* came on the stricken vessel and rescued them. The smack worth £120 and cargo worth £53 were lost off the Old Head on 17 August 1860.[131]

Adelaide: February 1862

The *Adelaide* was a sloop out of the port of Cork bound for Clonakilty with a cargo of 52 tons of Indian corn. Prior to setting out she had been windbound for more than two weeks in the vicinity of Crosshaven. On Thursday 6 February 1862 close to dusk, she lost her young deckhand and the jib as she endeavoured to round a headland (probably Black Head) near the narrowest point of the Old Head. She was observed by the lighthouse keepers after making her way into Holeopen Bay East in a stiff southeasterly wind, a bay which afforded no shelter in such a wind and was surrounded by precipitous cliffs. No assistance could be given as night closed in, and it was presumed that she had foundered with no hope of rescuing any survivors. This was the feeling that ensued for several days among the local populace given the conditions at the time. However, this was not the true story. The *Adelaide* had wedged itself into one of several sea caves that penetrate the narrowest point of the peninsula and run through from Holeopen Bay East to Holeopen Bay West. The vessel lodged itself halfway through one of the 200-yard-long and 30-foot-high caves. The captain John Mahony and a seaman named Driscoll were at this time the only men aboard. They endeavoured on Friday to escape from their watery prison. However, this attempt proved unsuccessful as the water pounded them on both sides. On Saturday, after another precarious night in this position, they placed two pieces of timber together and attempted to get out on the western side. In this attempt Driscoll, worn out by extreme exhaustion, fell from the timbers and was hauled back by Mahony. However he died immediately. Mahony, seeing nothing but certain death before him by remaining in the debris, and rapidly losing the use of his hands and feet made a final attempt to break free from the cave on Saturday afternoon. He swam and waded to some shelving rocks at the western mouth of the cave where he spent his third night. All Sunday was spent wading, swimming and scrambling around gullies and the bases of sharp and precipitous rocks. He spent the next night at the foot of a cliff less steep

130 *Cork Examiner*, 3 August 1857.
131 *Historic Shipwrecks of the East and West Cork Coast.*

than the others. The following morning, summoning his remaining strength for a last and final effort, he clambered up the two hundred foot slope. He was at this stage exhausted, starved, bruised and wounded and was taken into care by the lightkeeper. He went on to make a full recovery.[132]

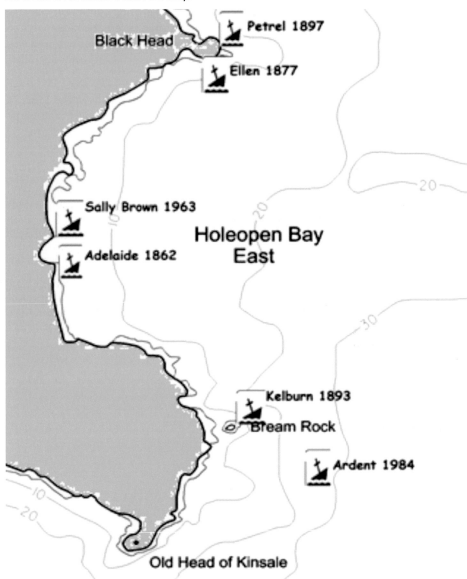

⚓ Fig 15: Known shipwreck locations between Black Head and the top of the Old Head. *Chart courtesy of Rob Jacob.*

---

132   *Cork Examiner,* 13 February 1862.

Louisiana: Went ashore on the Old Head on 11 January 1865. This 1,643-ton vessel carrying 500 passengers as well as general cargo was on a voyage from Liverpool to New York and had called to Queenstown to embark passengers. As the pilot departed outside Roches Point the steamship was shrouded in a cloak of fog which became very thick just at nightfall. The vessel soon went ashore in the vicinity of the Old Head. She was subsequently refloated and returned to Queenstown, where the passengers and cargo were transferred. The ship proceeded to Liverpool where it was declared a total loss after examination. The master named Asplet had his certificate suspended for six months.[133]

Childwickbury: Lost near the entrance to Kinsale Harbour on 15 November 1866. This fully rigged ship of 1,046 tons carrying a cargo of coal was on a voyage from Liverpool to Callao, under the command of Captain Joseph Braithwaite:

> Left Liverpool on 12 November carrying coal. The ship's compasses, of which there were two on deck, one in a binnacle on the break of the poop, the other aft in front of the wheel, were found to vary considerably, so a third compass was placed immediately behind but in contact with the forward binnacle. In this position they differed as much as two points or more than the steering compass. On the 14th, the Smalls were sighted and at 4pm a sounding found no bottom at 50 fathoms.
> Soon after this, the master felt unwell and left the deck in charge of the mate, telling him to keep the lead-line going every two hours. That evening thick fog set in and by midnight they were in thirty fathoms of which the master was informed, who gave orders to wear ship, but before this could be done she struck a rock and became a total wreck. The Court of Inquiry felt there were several points in which blame could be attached to the officer in charge. The placing of compasses so near to each other was bound to cause differences, and the ship should not have gone to sea without having them accurately tested. The Court did not regard the loss of the ship as arising from any neglect on the part of the captain.[134]

133   E.J. Bourke, vol 1 p.121.
134   B.T & R. Larn, *Shipwreck Index of the Irish Coast.*

↕ Fig.16: The east side of the Old Head, including Holeopen Bay East. The Adelaide was lost in the site, marked by a yellow star on the extreme right of the image in 1862. The red star marks where the Kelburn went ashore in 1893. *Courtesy of Kevin Dwyer.*

Kingston: 6 January 1867

The following sinking was reported in the *Cork Examiner* on 17 January 1867:

> The following is the report of Captain Shaw, of the Annhence for Gabon (Africa):-"At noon, Jan 6th, Old Head of Kinsale, bearing northwest., 35 miles, saw a ship dismasted and signals of distress flying. Found her to be the *Kingston* of Liverpool, for Calcutta, cargo salt, 1,201 tons, in a sinking condition, the captain killed by the falling of the mast, and several of the crew disabled. The chief mate requested me to lay by him for the night, and I agreed to do so. At 4pm the signals of distress were repeated; again bore down upon her; mate requested me to take them on board, which I did, and had them with me from the 6th until the 11th, when I landed them at Queenstown.

Maid of the Mill: Went ashore and lost at the Old Head on 23 January 1867. This 182-ton brig was bound from Dover to Cardiff.[135]

Harvest Queen: This barque was lost off the Old Head on 30 January 1867. The 374-ton vessel under Captain Matthews was on a voyage from Swansea to Baltimore carrying a cargo of coal.[136]

135   www.Irishshipwrecks.com
136   B.T. & R. Larn, *Shipwreck Index of the Irish Coast.*

THE WRECK OF THE *STONEWALL JACKSON* IN 1867

The *Stonewall Jackson* was a 461-ton barque of composite build – that is, wood on a metal frame. She was built at Liverpool in 1862-3, first registered in Liverpool in 1863, register moved to Cork in 1864. She was owned by James Humby of Liverpool who owned another vessel of the same name. This vessel was also a barque, of 429 tons, registered in Liverpool too, and was lost in 1871. A barque of this size would normally have had a crew of about eighteen men. The captain, named Russell, had his wife and one child on board.

This ship left Liverpool on 22 January on a voyage to the Cape of Good Hope carrying coal. The weather of January, February and March of that year was characterised by hurricanes in the Atlantic. Many ships were lost, some off the south coast of Ireland. When the *Stonewall Jackson* under Captain Russell appeared off Kinsale seven weeks after leaving Liverpool, the assumption was that the she must have suffered damage in a storm and turned back.

> About five o'clock on the evening of Monday (18th), when the outward bound Inman Steamer *City of Manchester* was passing the Old Head of Kinsale about three miles off the Bulman Buoy, the coastguard at the Old Head observed her take a crew off a large ship, with white ports, which was in a sinking state, and then proceed upon her voyage. The coastguard reported the matter at Kinsale, and Messrs Scott and Co.'s pilot boat the *Petrel*, which happened to be in the harbour, put to sail in search of the distressed vessel, nothing had been seen or heard up to an advanced hour last evening.

This report, however, proved to be inaccurate, as the crew of the *Stonewall Jackson* were still aboard their own ship and had not been removed as first reported.

> On the 18th of March when the *City of Manchester* was on an outbound voyage to New York it encountered a barque with the British ensign hoisted off Kinsale about 3-30pm and the vessel appeared to be disabled. Captain Jones bore down on the vessel. In reply to a signal of what was required, the captain (Russell) of the barque said his vessel was the *Stonewall Jackson* of Liverpool and that she was sinking. An offer was made to take the distressed crew on board the steamer, but it was declined. Captain Jones then asked if he should take the vessel in tow. To this Captain Russell consented but refused to send his own boat for the towline. Under the circumstances No 4 boat of the steamer was launched and the chief officer along with six crewmen pulled alongside the barque and succeeded in making fast a cable. The boat and boat crew of Captain Jones's tender had a narrow escape when coming alongside the Steamer from the Barque. The boat was swamped, but the men were saved. The vessel was then taken in tow, but sometime afterwards the line parted and a fresh manila rope was put on board the barque together with an extra cable. The steamer then proceeded at half speed and the night becoming very dark, though the Old Head light was visible.[137]

When off Kinsale Harbour the tow rope was found to be slack and, on being tested, was found to be detached from the other vessel. Upon examination, it was found that the towline had not snapped, the eye holes being perfect. Captain Jones and his officers, thinking the barque no longer needed assistance as the ropes had clearly been cast loose by those on board the *Stonewall Jackson,* proceeded on his voyage. 'With the exception of a piece of wreckage being washed ashore near Kinsale and being identified as part of the barque, nothing has since been heard of her and there can be no doubt Captain Russell from motives of his own, probably a desire to save salvage money cast off the tow rope when off the mouth of Kinsale Harbour and attempted to enter and on doing so came to grief with all on board.'[138]

The *Cork Examiner* of the 25 March 1867 reports the following:

> 'It is very much regretted that the information originally published in reference to this sad occurrence is not correct, as instead of the crew having as stated been all saved by the *City of Manchester,* many lives undoubtedly been lost. The wreck occurred about eight o' clock on the evening of the 18th, on the rocks of Duneen, about midway between the Old Head and Kinsale Harbour. It goes on to say that there is little reason to hope that even one escaped. Four bodies have been washed ashore-one apparently, that of the captain; another from the fact of having worn a wedding ring, evidently that of a married woman, is supposed to be that of the captain's wife. Mr. Coroner Horgan held an inquest on the bodies yesterday. Nothing has been heard from the owners or underwriters, who, no doubt, are under the impression that the crew have been saved'.

Edward J.Bourke in his excellent 'Shipwrecks of the Irish Coast' incorrectly names her as being an American Ship involved in smuggling. In the records for the mid-19th century there are numerous ships of this name. Bourke mentions that two of the bodies were interred at Belgooly cemetery. Could they have possibly been those of Captain Russell and his wife? This assumption is based upon the surmise that the bodies were not in a state of decay in order to have been transported as far as Belgooly for burial. According to local tradition in Dooneen, the bodies were interred in a grave on the cliff top field. There is a raised area in this field today to the south of *Cuas Buídhe,* which possibly marks the final resting place of the crew of the *Stonewall Jackson.* The placename of the inlet where the bodies were found reveals to us a vital piece of information as to the location of the nearby wreck site. The wreck site is a short distance to the west of this inlet. This place known to the older generation of Old Head people as *Cuaisín na nDaoine Báite* (little cove of the drowned people).It is a rocky cove located in the northwest corner of Bullen's Bay on the headland at the south side of *Cuas Buidhe.*

One rather puzzling aspect about this vessel is that the ship's crew agreements, held in the National Archives of Ireland, do not have a Captain Russell or a lady on the agreement, yet the press reports clearly state that he was the captain of the ship. Furthermore, the later report states that the bodies of Russell and his wife were washed up on the shore. The document clearly states that she was lost near Kinsale. This is further complicated by the fact that three different vessels belonging to the original Liverpool owner each had the same name, the name *Stonewall Jackson* being a very iconic one that lingers long in the memory. Jimmy Lawton, late of Dooneen Lower, who lived a short distance from the fatal shore often remarked that anytime you had a bad gale from the east at night, the old people would say they could hear the wails of the shipwrecked sailors pleading fo help.

138 Ibid.

⚓ Fig.17: *Cuaisín na nDaoine Báite* is marked by a red star. It was a short distance to the left of the star that fatal vessel *Stonewall Jackson* was lost in 1867. The untilled patch of land on the clifftop has a small mound where according to local tradition the bodies of the victims were interred. The yellow star represents the *Repartere* which went ashore in 1838. *Courtesy of Kevin Dwyer.*

It is not too often that we are given exact location for shipwrecks of this period, given the press's lack of local knowledge. All too often the reports state 'lost near Kinsale' or 'lost near Courtmacsherry'. This case is an exception and it came about as a result of a conversation between a local diver and another man steeped in local folklore. The combination of *Dinnseanchas* (lore of place), underwater archaeology and historic reports helped identify this lonesome resting place. The preservation of local minor placenames such as this one, give us a small window into past events that we may otherwise have no information about. This topic is dealt with in the final chapter.

Pollux: 25 March 1867

The period surrounding the loss of this vessel was characterised by very strong gales, both from the east and west, with low pressure systems passing to both the south and north of Ireland in a succession of fronts. Contempory reports from the time state that the weather was the worst for at least a quarter of a century. Ice hulks such as the *Pollux* were regular visitors to Kinsale during this time; they were a constant presence in the harbour during the spring mackerel fishery. This fishery usually started during

⚓ Fig.18: *Cuaisín na nDaoine Báite* in strong easterly wind. It was here that some of the bodies of the crew of the *Stonewall Jackson* were washed up in 1867.   *Author's Collection.*

the second week of March and reports from this period give a good indication of the frequency of this:

> A Norwegian barque arrived (April 17th) with 500 tons of ice, which brought to 3,500 tons the amount imported to Kinsale since the season had opened.[139]

It also highlights the importance of Kinsale as a fishery centre at the time, with a huge amount of vessels coming and going on a daily basis. The following report appeared in the press a few days after the loss of the above vessel:

> On Monday evening, during the fierce gale from the SSW, a Norwegian barque, the *Pollux*, 430 ton register, laden with ice for the Kinsale Fishery, was driven from her moorings in the harbour and dashed to pieces - literally to matchwood - on the rocks. The barque was an old vessel, but in perfectly seaworthy condition. She had a crew of fifteen men, all told; including the captain (Tenneson) and two mates. Her cargo consisted of about 800 tons of ice, which was consigned to the South of Ireland Fishing Company, for the purpose of packing fish for the markets. She was 24 days out of Christiana (Oslo), and had been thirteen days knocking about off the coast, unable to approach the harbour of Kinsale (her destination), in the thick and stormy weather that prevailed at that time. At length, after having her foretopsail blown away, one of the boats swept from the davits, and some damage done to her bulwarks, the ship fell in with a pilot-boat, three miles off the Old Head about noon, on Sunday, and from her receiving a pilot, who brought the barque into port. It was then low water, and as the barque drew twenty foot of water, it was impossible to bring her in past the bar-which runs across the harbour near Charles Fort. The pilot had, therefore, to bring her inside Prehane Point, where she was exposed to a southerly wind. She had two anchors down, however, and if the wind had not stiffened into the fierce gale it did, she probably would have ridden it out in perfect safety. The pilot left her immediately after she had been moored, the starboard anchor being then out. The wind increased on Monday, and the captain brought the pilot on board to see if he could do anything, by running her further up the bay or otherwise, to render her position less perilous. The wind however, was too violent for the vessel being moored, and as the only precaution that could be taken the port anchor was let go, in order to keep the vessel clear of the shore. The gale increasing, and with the strain on the cables of the *Pollux*, the port chain parted about seven o'clock on Monday evening. It should be remembered then that the gale from the south-southwest, blew clear into the harbour, so that the otherwise landlocked portion of the anchorage was of no avail for the barque in her then situation. The sea drove in with such immense force, heaving and tossing the barque in such a manner, that despite her double moorings, it could scarcely be expected that she would long withstand its violence. Captain Tennesson and his crew remained by her, although their peril every moment increased. At seven p.m., her port hawser parted, and the barque began to drift (dragging her remaining anchor) towards the eastern shore, upon which the sea was breaking with a tremendous roar, sending the spray far over the cliff, which is there very lofty. The captain endeavoured to relieve the strain upon the remaining cable by paying it out, till there was 60 fathoms in the water, and the vessel was within a cable's length of the land. At this part of the harbour from Charles Fort seaward, there is a series of low-lying rocks that put out, nearly one hundred feet into the bay, and towards these the *Pollux* was approaching. At length about eight p.m. intense darkness adding to the fearful peril of her crew's situation, the *Pollux*, still dragging her anchor, struck the rocks heavily, and in a few minutes after she bumped again, she bumped twice again, so that she vibrated in every part and the noise of crushing timbers was heard. Immediately she began to fill, and it was by superhuman exertion the long boat was lowered into the surf, and the captain and his crew scrambled into it, without having time to take with them more than one or two articles. Even

the captain's chronometer and the seamen's clothes could not be removed. It was half-past eight when they left her and with some difficulty pulled up the bay, landing at Denis's Quay about ten o'clock... When the captain was enabled to return by land to the scene of the disaster, with the coastguard after midnight, all that was visible of his 500 ton barque was a fragment of the hull...The cargo was estimated to be worth £1000 and the vessel was insured.[140]

The reporter seems to be using a bit of poetic licence here in describing the 'very lofty' cliffs, of which there are none in the harbour. It seems he may have got his report from a crew member and most likely he had not visited the scene of the disaster at all. The skipper of the vessel may have been planning initially to enter the harbour during a period of spring tides, especially in the month of March, when the greatest springs will occur as a new or full moon, which is in perigee, occurs near the equinox, and combines with high water and calm conditions. This stage of the tides would have given him a depth of between 25 to 30ft north of Money Point and in the channel. However, if the tides were of the neap variety and there was a swell (which there most certainly was), then the vessel constrained by her draft of 20ft and a possible depth of 20-24ft in the same area of the channel at high water, was in a very precarious position. The above article states that the pilot boarded the vessel at 12 noon and got to the harbour's mouth at low water. We can only estimate how long it took to get from three miles off the Old Head to the harbour (over an hour in normal circumstances), which would make low water at approximately 1.30-2pm, and would indicate that the tides were close to the height of the springs. He may have just missed the biggest tides: a prudent skipper, with the constraints on his draft that he had, would in all probability have planned to enter Kinsale at the highest tide. Depth would only have been an issue in one part of the channel, the part known as 'the bar', which is approximately two cables wide, going right across the channel (east to west) and extends south from Charles Fort for three cables. A rule of thumb to bear in mind in relation to Kinsale, is that when low water occurs around midday the tides are generally near or at springs and when high water occurs around midday the tides are neaps and generally weak. In hindsight, he was in a very unenviable position, and the only place he may have got a bit of a lee before approaching the harbour was in close, just on the north side of Black Head, or in *Cistin* in the southwest corner of Holeopen Bay East, a very calm place and aptly named, given it was a popular spot for local fishing vessels to prepare a meal when the wind was in the prevailing direction (southwest). In summary, the vessel could only have passed over the bar at high water on a spring tide in calm conditions. However, if the weather conditions at the time are to be believed, there was probably a bit of a heave on the shore in that area due to the strong easterly wind that wrecked the *Stonewall Jackson* a couple of days previously. To have anchored, as is suggested, inside Prehane Point was very high risk. It may be that the writer mistakenly took Prehane Point to mean the Eastern Point, a common mistake with those unfamiliar with the area, and the vessel ended up on the shore somewhere in the vicinity of Middle Cove. The risk factor involved here was that the wind could easily back around from the south-south-west a couple of points and one would be in serious trouble. Before the advent of steam engines and weather forecasts, every voyage was providential.

140   *Cork Examiner*, 29 March 1867.

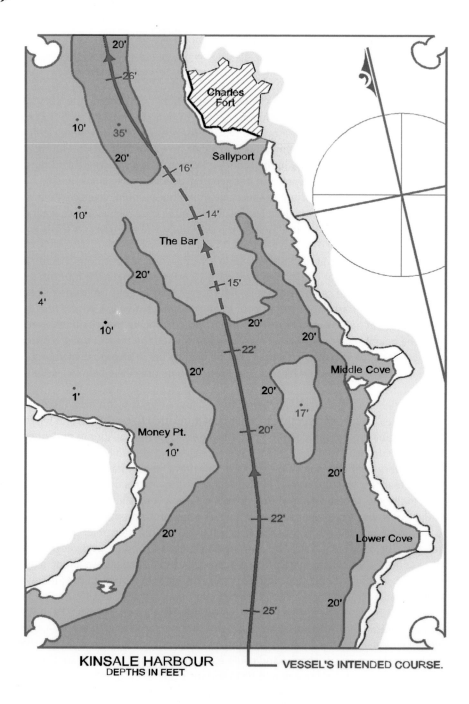

KINSALE HARBOUR
DEPTHS IN FEET

—— VESSEL'S INTENDED COURSE.

⚓ Fig.19: Illustration by Rob Jacob showing the intended route of the *Pollux*.

ICE PICKS

ICE PICKS
WERE USED
TO HANDLE
BLOCKS OF
ICE, WHICH
CAME FROM
·NORWAY·

Fig.20: Ice picks as used on Norwegian ice luggers- currently housed in the Kinsale Museum. *Courtesy of Kinsale Museum.*

Nancy: Lost off the Sovereign Islands on 9 July 1867. This 17-ton Oysterhaven fishing smack was anchored off the Sovereign Islands at about 1 am. They were fishing for hake and had about 35 fish aboard when their vessel was run down by the trans-Atlantic liner *Nebraska* which immediately sank her. Four of the crew were drowned and three recovered from the water. David Hogan and David Corcoran survived, but Patrick Murphy later died on board.[141]

Cossipore: Lost 30 miles south of the Old Head in wind conditions west-northwest force 12 on 8 January 1870. This fully-rigged ship of 1,226 tons was carrying a cargo of salt under master Beynon and 27 crew.[142]

Aeron Lass: Friday 13 October 1871

On Friday the thirteenth, at around 10.30pm a schooner named the *Aeron Lass* of Aberystwyth, under the command of Captain Owens, ran ashore at the White Strand, on the west side of the Old Head of Kinsale. She was outward bound from Newport with a cargo of coal for Queenstown (Cobh). The timely arrival of the local coastguards, under chief boatman John O'Donovan and his crew of five men, ensured that the crew, five in number, were safely hauled ashore by the rocket apparatus at 3am. A message was dispatched to Kinsale by Captain Carter to the Customs House officers, who quickly appeared on the spot to evaluate the situation. The vessel was deemed to be in a dangerous position. The captain thanked the coastguard but declined further assistance. On Sunday morning at low water the captain was in town and the mate called on the coastguards to assist him as the locals began to salvage the wreckage. However, when the captain arrived back on the scene he ordered the coastguards away. He was astonished to find the wreckage was still being further plundered. Some items including the ship's boat came ashore and were broken up in a short time, the pieces later taken away. He then went to the police in Ballinspittle who took charge of the wreck. The ship ended up a total wreck.[143]

The following week's edition of *The West Cork Eagle & County Advertiser* on 28 October 1871 had a letter penned by the chief boatman of the Old Head lifesaving crew.

> Sir,-The Aeron *Lass* stranded on the White Strand on the west side of the Old Head of Kinsale, which was inserted in last Saturday's issue as being robbed and plundered by the country people of Courceys, so far as being robbed and plundered is perfectly true, but, representing the inhabitants of a large tract of country amounting to 3,500 (within one police district) as charged with this wanton and barbarous depredation is most derogatory to the majority. There are only about twenty persons connected with the townlands of Garrylucas, Coolbawn, Ballincurrig and the Old Head, who are the transgressors, but within those places I must say, there are true honest, charitable and sympathizing people. It is monstrous to think that a large district should be represented as guilty of the acts of a few, for there is no community without its rotten member. Now, sir, it is privately understood

141 www.corkshipwrecks.net
142 B.T & R. Larn, *Shipwreck Index of the Irish Coast.*
143 *West Cork Eagle & County Advertiser.* 21 October 1871.

and whispered to charge this pillage on the parish, as malicious injury, but let those that are entrusted with the preservation of peace and order (I mean the police and coastguards) speak out and testify the knowledge they possess, and then the public will see the people of Courceys must not be charged in general with the crimes of a few. The captain and mate of the vessel have identified the wolves, and, as they have done so the police will have sufficient grounds for their legal action, especially as they and the coastguards know the robbers. If they do not, let the authorities institute a sworn investigation, and find out the delinquents, so that the honestly disposed people of so large a district should not be saddled with a heavy tax for malicious injury; also, let the honest people of the district show their disapproval of such a wanton and inhuman act, aided by their worthy parish priest and curate, who spoke with touching sympathy and Christian feeling respecting the cast ashore strangers, and strongly denouncing the ruffainly acts of those who plundered them. There will be no doubt but the offenders will be justly punished, which may give them a sense of honesty. Those wreck-robbers have no act or part with the people of Courceys: they must have descended from a class which we are ashamed to have as belonging to our part of the country.

I am, sir, yours,

J.D., Courceys.

{It is with much pleasure we publish the out-spoken letter of "J.D.," as we could not imagine that the people of Courceys, in general, could be guilty of the heinous offence of robbing those who are already deprived of much of their property by the inclement ocean. We should be sorry that such a stain should rest on a people who are noted for honesty, kindness, and hospitality, and feel glad that the offence complained of rests only on the "black sheep" which are found in every flock"}

The Coastguard acted as a reserve for the navy, protecting the Revenue's interests and defending the coast against smugglers. They ensured that wrecks were not illegally plundered and assisted the police in discovering illicit stills. None of these activities endeared the Coastguard to the local population.[144]

⚓ Fig.21: Many vessels have come to grief on the White Strand at the base of the Old Head peninsula; amongst those discussed in this study are the *Aeron Lass* 1871, *Guelf of Quebec* 1891, *and Rob Roy* 1907. The troop ships *Lord Melville* and *Boadicea* were lost on the northern end of this strand at the *Curlán* in 1816. *Courtesy of Kevin Dwyer.*

144 *Step back in Time in Courtmacsherry.* Courtmacsherry Harbour Lifeboat Station History Group, 2014, p.67.

Rambler: This brigantine was lost off the Old Head in severe easterly gales on 1 February 1873.[145]

Dasher: Lost near Kinsale on 1 February 1873. A schooner of 70 tons bound from Port Dinorwic (Wales) to Cork with a cargo of roofing slates. The master's name was John Hughes.

> Left Dinorwic on 30.January carrying a cargo of slates. About midnight the following day, during a SSE gale the fore trestle-trees were carried away, bringing with them the foretopmast, rendering the topsail useless. The vessel was hauled to the wind, and continued thus till morning. About 10 a.m. on 1. February, the Old Head of Kinsale was made, and the crew endeavoured to reach Kinsale Harbour, but in doing so, a heavy sea struck the vessel which did much damage and rendered her unmanageable. She then drifted towards the shore, large quantities of water finding their way into the fore hatch, which had been stove in and which it was found impossible to recover. Finding the vessel rapidly filling with water and still drifting towards the shore, the crew took to their boat and after much difficulty succeeded in landing. The court were of the opinion that notwithstanding the age of the vessel (built 1805), which had gone under extensive repair at different times, and was in good seaworthy condition, her loss was attributed to stress of weather and that no blame could be attached to her master or crew.[146]

Olive: Lost twenty five miles southeast of the Old Head on 21 March 1873. This 22-ton dandy from the Isle of Man was lost when she collided with another vessel in a southwesterly force six on the fishing grounds.[147]

Laura: Lost after developing a leak in an easterly force 9, thirty three miles south of the Old Head on 6 November 1873. The vessel, a schooner, was on a voyage from Newport to Queenstown with a cargo of 140 tons of coal. The 58-ton vessel was built in 1792 and carried a crew of three.[148] The crew were rescued and the schooner sank.[149]

Hercules: February 1874.

The *Hercules* went ashore at Bogstown midway between Howe Strand and Garretstown Strand. The vessel was a German barque, bound in ballast from Barrow-in-Furness to Cardiff for coals. When off the Smalls, she was caught in an easterly gale and driven before the weather to the west. Straining in the heavy seas, she began to leak and the sand, which acted as ballast, clogged the pumps. The captain Parov attempted to steer the unmanageable vessel to Waterford but failed to do so. She ran before the weather, and as the bilges filled up more, the rolling sand burst her decks. On Wednesday morning, she hit the rocks in the northern shore of Courtmacsherry Bay. The mate Nicholas Strum jumped overboard in the hope of carrying a line to the shore, but was lost in the raging sea. A boat was put out but this was immediately swamped. The vessel broke up and it is thought that only one crewman survived. The captain, mate and nine other seamen perished. The survivor, Carl Kooks, survived by catching

---

145   www.corkshipwrecks.net
146   B.T & R. Larn, *Shipwreck Index of the Irish Coast.*
147   Ibid.
148   Ibid.
149   *Historic Shipwrecks of the East and West Cork Coast.*

a floating spar, supported by this he was flung on to a rock. He was kindly treated by a man named John Harrington into whose home he wandered, and while there he was well treated by Dr Hegarty, the Hon Colonel Bernard and Mr Stawell.[150]

The spot today is marked by a cleft in the rock and is known to the people of that part of the coast as 'German Cove'.[151]

⚓ Fig 22: Foghorn from the *Hercules. Courtesy of Paddy O'Sullivan*

150   *Cork Examiner.* 16 February 1874.
151   Pádraigh O'Donovan personal communication.

⚓ Fig.23: Bell of the *Hercules*. *Courtesy of Paddy O'Sullivan*

⚓ *Fig.24: Cuas na Marbh. This evocative name illustrates the loss of life here in 1874. Author's Collection.*

⚓ Fig.25: German Cove-it was here that Carl Kooks, the only survivor of the *Hercules* made his way to safety. The remains of John Harrington's home are a short distance to the left (east) of this image. *Courtesy of Michael Prior*

Abraham Lincoln: 11 February 1874

This barque-rigged ship went ashore on the same morning as the *Hercules* between Howe Strand and Garranfeen Strand only a little over a mile distant from the scene of the *Hercules* disaster. She was outward bound from Cardiff under Captain John Babista Benfante. The crew consisted of thirteen hands. She sailed on the 9th and at 4pm the next day, a strong gale began to blow and she was struck by several heavy seas, which carried away her bulwarks, boats and everything on deck. The crew immediately set to heaving the cargo overboard and the captain headed for the Irish coast. He sighted land at 10.30pm and, in spite of his exertion, the vessel grounded at 1.30am on Wednesday. Several of the crew who had tried to get a rope ashore were washed away by the waves. The vessel was further pushed up on to the rocky shore. The captain, his two mates and four crewmen escaped by clambering on to the shore and avoiding certain death. The same night there were numerous reports of ships perishing in the severe weather conditions.[152]

Secellia: This Carlingford fishing vessel was driven on to the rocks in poor weather on 13 March 1876.[153]

152   *Cork Examiner.* 16 February 1874.
153   Coleman O'Mahony, Fishing in 19th century Kinsale, *Journal of the Cork Historical & Archaeological Society.* Vol, 19, p.113-132.

Black Head 1877

On 28 August 1877, a dark cloud cast its shadow over the Old Head as a consequence of a fishing disaster that took the lives of five men from that peninsula.

The ill-fated vessel (*Ellen*) that left the cove at *Doras Breac* at 7am was an open four-ton fishing boat with five oars. The crew members were James Roche, John Nagle, John Collins, Tim Quinn, Jeremiah Quinn, Keane Connolly, Jeremiah Forde, Jeremiah Kingston, Patrick Minihane and James Coughlan.

John Nagle, a comfortably off farmer who had a great knowledge of local waters, was the helmsman as well as being part owner of the boat and its fishing gear. He resided in a house where today stands a farm shed belonging to Alan Coleman, just north of *Leabaidh a' Bháid* in the townland of Lispatrick Lower. He was about 60 years of age, the eldest of the crew.

The doomed boat went about its business of fishing off the Old Head until the crew returned to Holeopen Bay at 4pm for their dinner. They then set out for the fishing area again, passing the Old Head where they stayed until 7pm. The fishing was not very productive and they started for home.

Dr Hegarty of Ballinspittle stated that Nagle's death was caused by falling into the water in an exhausted condition. The jury under foreman Patrick O'Connell found a verdict accordingly. The second inquest was held the same day at the Old Head and the evidence given by Jeremiah Kingston, an able bodied young man, appeared as follows:

"I went fishing on that day with nine others. John Nagle was at the rudder. When we were going out in the morning we passed between the rock and the mainland. We were coming back about seven o'clock and we had some talk about going inside or outside the sunken rock and we tried to go inside it. The sea drew from the rock and we were swept over it and capsized at the other side. I and Jeremiah Quinn rose under the boat. When I found my head on the taut I went down and came to the surface" "When I came up I saw Quinn, Nagle and Roche were on the bottom of the boat. I made for it and got on. Old Nagle was washed off by a sea, but he rose again near the boat and I pulled him up. Forde came on then after being in the water for some time. The five others Coughlan, Keane Connolly, John Collins, Jim Roche and Patrick Minihane were still floating on the oars. John Collins was only two yards from the boat. He made no struggle and we saw him drowning. The others were inside us and appeared to be swimming to the shore. We drifted away to sea on the boat for half a mile and we saw Coughlan, Connolly, Roche and Minihane still floating on the oars. It then got too dark and we could see no more of them. Paddy Minihane had two oars, the others having one each. Coughlan (the deceased) and Kane Connolly were both good swimmers, were both outside the boat when we were upset, they told us to hang on and they would swim ashore and get assistance. They were both swimming well and Connolly had no oar then". "After upsetting old Nagle got on the boat, but was washed off when a sea came. He rose again and I gave him my leg and he held on to it for half an hour. At last I helped him on to the keel again. Another sea came and we were both washed off. We rose together and I got to the boat again, but I had a bad grip and Nagle was again holding my leg. He was pulling me off and I asked Roche who was near me to give me help or Nagle would pull me down. Another sea came. Which washed me up

> on the bottom and old Nagle completely over it to the other side. I didn't see him again. That after we had drifted a mile and a half to sea and when we were more than halfway back again on the tide. It was quite dark".[154]

Further evidence was given by Patrick Minihane who recorded what happened to the men left in the water with only oars for flotation assistance.

> "I was in the boat when she was upset and when I came to the surface I got an oar which supported me. I paddled about on it for a while and Jeremiah Forde had one also. He left it go and made for the boat. I took his oar and I had two and thought it better to keep them than go to the boat. I kept them both under my chest. I was drifting about for three hours on the oars. I kept away from the shore as I thought I would be killed on the rocks, there was such a sea. Coughlan and I were together until it got dark and I don't know where he went. I missed Connolly long before this. The only conversation we had before this was about keeping away from the rocks, because we thought we would all be killed if we tried to go ashore there. After three hours I was picked up by one of the boats that came out to us. I was not at all cold".[155]

The only injury to Coughlan was a mark on his right temple, which Dr Hegarty considered was caused by having been dashed off a rock, which rendered him unconscious. A verdict of drowning was returned. The people left the inquest to watch and pray for the still unrecovered bodies of John Collins, Tim Quinn and Keane Connolly who with Coughlan had become a hero to them having risked his life to get ashore and raise the alarm.[156]

It is quite remarkable that the inquest did not give any evidence of the weather

⚓ Fig.26: Sunken Rock breaking off the point of Black Head or the *Mionán* as it is known by the older generation. *Author's Collection.*

---

154   *Padraig Ó Maidín* articles.
155   Ibid.
156   Ibid.

conditions, tides or details of where exactly the event took place. The sunken rock referred to in the report of *West Cork Eagle & County Advertiser* was at Black Head. At the south-eastern tip of this headland is a sunken rock or *'bollán'*.

However, no one in their right mind would go inside this even in calm conditions given its proximity to the shore. It would serve no purpose and save no time or manpower no matter what direction one was going. I would hazard a guess that the sunken rock that the men spoke about going inside on their return voyage was the sunken rock at *'Carraig na Rón'* midway along the shore at Bullen's Bay. If one was returning to the cove at *Doras Breac* by going inside this rock, the journey could be shortened a little bit. These two sunken rocks are the only hazardous ones on the east side of the Old Head. While the newspaper reports suggest Black Head, but the inquest's mention of the sunken rock may not have referred to the Black Head *'bollán'* at all, but the aforementioned rock further north outside *Doras Breac*. It may be that hitting the sunken rock at Black Head was providential, rather than an attempt to go inside it. Further conclusive evidence is recorded in the following newspaper report from the time:

'At half past seven pm, while passing a sunken rock outside a bluff headland called Black Head.......a huge sea rolled over the rock striking and capsizing the boat and sending her ten occupants struggling for their life into the angry element. Five, including the skipper managed to get on the boat which lay bottom upward; one man named Collins sank immediately to rise up no more. A young man named Jas. Collins whose extraordinary swimming feats inspired both himself and his companions in distress with the hope that he would be able to safely gain the shore and send them speedy relief........he was dashed against the rocks and killed. James Coughlan followed Connolly, but he likewise failed in his attempt. The boat drifted along in a strong ebb tide till she reached a point about a half a mile distant, where she got into an eddy which drew her nearer to the shore and brought her back again half the distance. Here, as if under the guidance of providence, she made a stand where the cries which her living burthen were able to faintly utter, were heard by a young man named William Manning who was in the neighbourhood........It was now ten o'clock and the moon was just rising above yonder hill-top and soon shed her silvery light upon the face of the deep, enabling Manning to see from the top of the cliff the tiny object which for two and a half hours was the sport of the waves. Manning who up to that was doubtful whether the screams he heard were not those of some fishermen that may have been quarrelling in some fishing boats far away in the distance, now became alive to the real nature of the case and whistled to let them know the calls for help were then repeated with as much vigour as the strength of the drowned sufferers could afford. He went at the top of his speed till he arrived at the Old Head village (*Doras Breac*) where he gave the alarm and soon succeeded in getting two boats underway.... But they arrived immediately after poor Nagle had succumbed to exhaustion and dropped into a watery grave, thus completing the number of five victims. The first picked up was Patrick Minihane who had an oar under each arm.... He was in a very exhausted condition and became partially insensible when taken into the boat. The boats that rendered this timely aid belong to a Mr Calnan and Mr Dempsey....It may be mentioned that the same Wm Manning was the means once before of saving the life of one of the survivors James Roche. It is hardly necessary to say that his conduct is now worthy of the recognition of the Humane Society, for to him undoubtedly the following five men owe their lives: Jeremiah Ford, Jas Roche, Jeremiah Kingston, Jeremiah Quinn and Patrick Minihane. Those who have been lost are - John Nagle, farmer aged 60, J.Collins, labourer, aged 30 and married leaves a wife and three children; J. Coughlan aged 25, not married; Timothy Quinn aged 22 and Keane Connolly, age 26 unmarried. Beside the loss of five lives, the loss of the boat and seine is set down at £100; and it is a remarkable fact that that one man belonging to each of the five joint owners of the boat and net was drowned'. [157]

A few observations from the reports on the incident need clarification. The *West Cork Eagle* report indicated that the boat drifted south towards another headland (probably the *Beann Lao*) where the old lighthouse stands and then drifted halfway back towards the shore in an eddy. This is suggestive of Holeopen Bay East, where there are eddies, and the tide is less predictable than outside the line of the headlands to the north and south of the bay. The fact that William Manning's name was called out for assistance by the victims gives us further clarification of their approximate position. He was a resident at the castle bawn wall as were all his people before him. I would venture to suggest that the men had no intention of going inside the *'Bollán'* at Black Head (also known as the *Mionnán*). The distance between the rock and shore is only about 30ft. The question of going inside the sunken rock prompts a couple of questions. Firstly, how familiar was young Kingston (who mentioned a discussion about going inside a sunken rock in the inquest) with the local coastline? None of the men were full-time fishermen and some may have only fished very occasionally. This could have been one of a number of sunken rocks on the homeward passage. The sunken rocks at *Carraig na Rón, Carraigbreda* and the *Bollán* in Bullen's Bay could all be cut inside as a shortcut home to the cove. Bream Rock (not a sunken rock, but with a narrow channel on the inside) nearer to the present day lighthouse, would often be passed on the inside by mariners with a good local knowledge of the area. If one was coming from the fishing grounds west or south of the Old Head in a small vessel such as that in question, one could avoid much of the strong ebb tide by cutting inside this channel. Approaching the sunken rock at Black Head from all points between east and west-southwest, on course for Bullen's Bay and home, it makes absolutely no sense that they would have gone inside the rock. Today, the only people who venture inside this rock are kayakers and small lobster boats hauling pots in very calm weather. I would conclude by suggesting that they were heading north for home, passed too close or misjudged the rock and were fatally swept over it. The London *Daily Telegraph* reported on the tragedy. It wrote very disparagingly about the habits of the local Kinsale fishermen, The *Telegraph* reported very inaccurately about the event and the *West Cork Eagle* retorted vigorously:

> 'All in West Cork who read the details of the lamentable boat accident at the Old Head, which have been published, had no difficulty in understanding that the boat which the *Telegraph* has magnified into a fishing smack was none other than an open six-oar yawl of about 20 ft. keel, with a crew of ten men who set out on shoal water fishing with a seine, which is only adapted for that purpose. Leaving for the present the unfounded statement of the *Telegraph*, that for a long time the Old Head has been an evil omen for the Kinsale fishermen's wives, we must give the statement – which it was in Courtmacsherry Bay the boat capsized – the flattest contradiction. The catastrophe occurred between the Kinsale Head lighthouse and the Coastguard Station, some four or five miles nearer Kinsale

Harbour than Courtmacsherry Bay and on a fine calm night. Nor were the crew of the ill-fated boat Kinsale fishermen, as the *Telegraph* states. They were merely farm labourers, the skipper himself being a farmer, who went out on the fatal night in the hope of catching scad or other small fish that may fall into their hands. They capsized by keeping too near a shoal rock, which was known to be dangerous.... The gear and the wreckage with which the Old Head men went down had no existence except in the imaginative brain of the writer in the untruthful columns of the *Telegraph*.[158]

In the days that followed, much searching of the shore was carried out by locals and the coastguards for the missing bodies. The following was reported by the press on 15 September of that year:

Intelligence just to hand states that a body supposed to be one of those lost in the Old Head boat accident, has been picked up at Oysterhaven this (Thursday) evening, by the Coast-Guards. Assuming that this is one of the ill-fated crew it makes the third body now recovered. There has been a coroner's inquest held at the Old Head on Wednesday, on the body of the skipper, John Nagle, which was picked up at the Galley Head and on the body of Jeremiah Coughlan which was found quite close to the disaster. The evidence of Patrick Minihane, who was rescued with the two oars keeping him afloat, was truly touching. He said that he was in the state of mind that he saw eternity before his eyes, but felt quite warm all the time he was in the water. The bodies still missing are those of Jeremiah Collins, Timothy Quinn and Keane Connolly. A subscription has been started for the families of those who have lost their lives, and we believe about £30 has been already collected.[159]

Seven days later, another press release confirmed another body had been found.

Information to hand from the Old Head states that the body of Timothy Quinn, one of the five men drowned on the night of the 28th last, has been recovered quite close to where the accident occurred. The features were quite unrecognisable, all the flesh having been removed by the action of the water as well as from any exposed part of the body. This makes the fourth body now recovered, and that of Jeremiah Collins is now the missing one. It is stated that a liberal response to the appeal which is now being made to the public on behalf of the families of the deceased, is making very substantial additions to the relief fund, and considering the activity of several members of the committee, and especially the hon. secretary, Mr J. Dempsey.[160]

It is not known if the body of Jeremiah Collins was ever found. In all probability it was not recovered; close scrutiny of local publications from that time does not reveal any information. The last press release relating to the tragedy came on 20 October:

The subscription list in aid of the Old Head relief fund having been closed, the commissioners met in the board-room of the Town Commissioners, Kinsale, on Friday evening, and the 12th inst., for the purpose of dividing the sum collected. Mr. B. Popham, manager of the Munster Bank, and chairman of the committee, presided, and the other members present were-N.J. Walsh, Hon. Treasurer; Jeremiah Dempsey, Hon. Secretary, Town Clerk; Dr. J. C. Nunan, chairman Town Commissioners, and H.C; Dr Dunn, T.C., and H.C.; Rev E. Murphy, R.C.C. According to the statement laid before the meeting by the secretary and treasurer the amount of subscriptions received was £113. 7s.6d, and after consideration of the circumstances of the sufferers, the

158   Ibid, 8 September 1877.
159   Ibid, 15 September 1877.
160   Ibid, 22 September 1877.

following distribution was made: - To Mrs Quinn, £10. Mrs Connolly, £10;Mrs Coughlan £10, Mrs Nagle, the widow of John Nagle, being in better circumstances than the others, got £8; and the following sums were allocated for the survivors:-J.Ford,£2; J.Roche,£1; J. Quinn,£1; P.Minihane, £1; and J.Kingston, £1. In addition to the £2 already awarded by the R.N.L.I, through Mr .Tomkins to William Manning in recognition of his timely aid to the survivors, the committee considered that he was entitled to £1 of the money at their disposal. It was determined to place the balance remaining, after paying expenses of publishing lists of subscriptions in the hands of the chairman and the parish priest of Courceys in trust for the benefit of the orphans of Jeremiah Collins, to be given at such times and in such a way as they may think fit.[161]

The descendants of some of the crew still live in the area today. Keane Connolly was a grand-uncle of the late Jim Connolly of Ballymackean, Old Head. His daughters, Ann and Margaret, still live on the Old Head today. In the 1901 census, Patrick Minihane of Kilcoleman, Old Head, a survivor of the tragic event, was 65 years of age, and lived with his son Dan, aged 30, and daughter Mary, aged 26. A family of that name lived there until recent times. Jeremiah Quinn, also aged 65, and from the same townland, had a son, William, and two daughters, Catherine and Hanna. Their descendants still live in Kilcoleman today. Jeremiah Kingston lived in Upper Lispatrick, near where Pat Lawton lives today.[162] He and his descendants were gone from the area in the 1901 census. The owner of the ill-fated boat is given as P. Connell of Kinsale.[163]

Francesca Curro: Lost after a collision with the *Malta* off the Old Head on 8 October 1877. This Genoan barque of 551 tons was en route from Philadelphia to Queenstown, carrying a cargo of Indian corn under Captain Monteri. The vessel carried a crew of fifteen and one passenger. The weather conditions at the time were good.[164]

161   Ibid, 20 September 1877.
162   J.P. Downing personal communication.
163   *Historic Shipwrecks of the East & West Cork Coast.*
164   B.T. & R. Larn, *Shipwreck Index of the Irish Coast.*

Chapter IV: 1878-1900

Mary Lily: 2 April 1878

Reported lost on 2 April severe weather conditions that occurred at this time:

> Intelligence reaching Kinsale on Wednesday evening that another fishing boat, called the *Mary Lily*, of Port St Mary, Isle of Man, was lost at 2am on Tuesday morning, on the Barrel Rocks, Kinsale, where she lost her nets in the late storm. The Skipper Robert Gill and three of his crewmen were saved, but the other four crew members were said to have perished.[165]

During this period of bad weather, some severe damage was done to the Kinsale fishing fleet. Many lost valuable nets and sustained damage to their vessels. The most extraordinary tale is told of the Courtmacsherry schooner *Alma*, which was blown nearly 200 miles off course. A continuously heavy sea swept her decks, making her little more than a floating wreck. The crew, however, secured themselves as best they could and were fortunately prevented from being washed away. The captain reckoned that she became totally disabled about 120 miles off Cape Clear. They were rescued by a passing ship, the *Annabella Clark*, on passage from Bilbao to Ardrossan. A couple of days later, this ship signalled a nearby vessel bound for Bristol and transferred the stricken fishermen on board the *Briton*. The Courtmacsherry men made a return home later that week on a ship bound from Bristol to Cork.

> 'The boat belonged to Mr Michael O'Driscoll of Courtmacsherry, a man of sterling worth and extraordinary enterprise, who gives employment to a great number of men all year round...He owns a fleet of fishing vessels operating just now in the mackerel fishing, some of them commanded by his own sons, while others are guided by intelligent men of the port. His youngest son was master of the 'Alma' and the crew were all sons or husbands of poor people in the immediate locality. They hoisted sail for the fishing ground on Monday 25th March, and among a multitudinous number of boats , plied their occupation until remuneratively till the night of Thursday 28th, when a gale unprecedentedly severe sprang up without the slightest warning note...Destruction, devastation and death reigned seemingly everywhere, and the morning of Friday dawned on pitiable scenes. Parents, wives, children thronged the heights commanding a sea-view...All had returned by Sunday, except the 'Alma'.[166]

Around 6 April, the crew arrived back in Cork and there was much rejoicing nationwide. The fishermen were dubbed 'the men who came back from the dead'. All the way from Cork City to Courtmacsherry there was much cheering and rejoicing for the eight returned men.

165 *West Cork Eagle & County Advertiser*, 6 April 1878.
166 *West Cork Eagle & County Advertiser*. 13 April 1878.

On Wednesday a telegram from Bristol from the skipper Jeremiah Driscoll, son to the proprietor of the ill-fated craft, announced the welcoming news of their safety... Preparations were inaugurated to give them a hearty *Céad Mile Failte* ...Every available car in Courtmacsherry and neighbourhood was hired, and a large contingent of pedestrians went to meet them as far as Bandon. They arrived in Timoleague led by the St Patrick's Total Abstinence Society Band and a goodly number of Bandon folk...All along the estuary bonfires blazed. All the vessels in the harbour were decked in their gayest bunting. A splendid display of fireworks was let off. The band after a tour of the village went to the residence of W.B.Leslie, Esq, and performed some excellent music. Returning to the village the members of the band were entertained by Mr Michael Driscoll and after spending a very gay evening, took their departure for merry Bandon town.[167]

Damage to the Kinsale Fishing Fleet: 6 April 1878

The following account appeared in the *West Cork Eagle & County Advertiser* on Saturday 6 April, 1878. The account was unfortunately all too commonplace given the constraints of nineteenth-century weather forecasting. Every press release about storms at sea was invariably followed by a litany of missing vessels and crews in the days and weeks that followed. Kinsale was in this respect very vulnerable given the huge mackerel fleet that fished from the port.

"The lamentable accounts which reached Kinsale on Saturday evening of the fishermen who had a hard battle for their lives shows that the public anxiety for their safety was well founded. One and all stated during the many years they have been coming to the fishery there has not been as much wholesale destruction of fishing gear as that which the furious gales of last Thursday night had wrought and the damage is lamentably aggravated by the loss of life reported of a boat with all hands". One of the Kinsale fishermen made the following statement to the writer.

"There are at least six of our boats which have been left without a stich of their train (string of drift nets), whilst others have lost half and others a third."

Speaking of the effect of such losses, he said

"I have known some of the poor men who have been among the heaviest sufferers, to have for the past seven years been saving up for the cost of their nets, and often starving themselves and their children to do so, and to be in one night without the fruit of seven years hard saving is quite enough to make the sufferer wish himself gone with them. I know many men as well as myself, who would not have cared to have shared the fate of those who were swept off the 'Dolly Varden.'

Similar statements have been made by Manx and Dubliners as regards the severity of the storm and the losses they have suffered. Many had to ride out the storm rather than part with their nets, and such as were able to haul them ran for Crookhaven, Baltimore and wherever else a place of safety could be reached. The names of the two men lost off the *Dolly Varden* are Peter Leonard and James Burns. Neither of them were married. There were four swept overboard by the tremendous sea which broke over the boat, but two were thrown back by a succeeding sea, and thus saved. No less than 130 boats have gone home with the loss of all their gear and the greater portion of those who remain will have to fish with half trains. The entire loss was estimated at £35,000, to say nothing of the

---

167   Ibid.

consequential loss which would far exceed the above, so that £70,000 was but a moderating sum to be charged against the storms of last Thursday night and Friday morning. The fine boat *Garryowen* owned by Dr. Dean of Kinsale, lost her whole train of nets, and one of her sails (presumably her mizzen sail) was blown away, thus sustaining an actual loss of over £200. The skipper of a Peel boat named *Maggie Madril* states that he saw the boat disappear after being struck by a heavy sea. He describes the boat as having her bottom painted a lead colour and riding in the storm with a white mizzen sail. He said that when struck by a fatal sea, he saw the traveller fly up to the masts top and then the boat which was about half the length of his train away (about half a mile) went down. The steamers that left the same evening with cargoes of fish for Milford Haven have reported the weather as the severest experienced for a long time and instead of making the run in fourteen hours as is usual, the run took twenty five hours. One is reported as having her bulwarks stove in and sustaining other slight injuries.

Further confirmation reached Kinsale that the fishing vessel, *Mary Lily*, of Port St Mary, Isle of Man, was lost at 2am on Tuesday morning on the Barrel Rocks in Courtmacsherry Bay. The skipper and three of the crew were saved, but four other crewmen are said to have perished.[168]

Other reports tell the tale of eight Courtmacsherry fishermen from the schooner *Alma* which was blown 200 miles off course. This incident has already been described. As a consequence of the events of that period the Lords of the Admiralty gave directions for the immediate erection of a storm drum signal at the Coastguard Station at Summercove for the benefit of the fishery. The chief officer of the Coastguard was to be supplied with information through telegrams from the Meteorological Department announcing impending storms.[169]

General Caulfield: Lost on the bar at Courtmacsherry on 12 January 1879. This barque of 650 tons was on course from New York to Dunkirk with a cargo of wheat. She carried a crew of eighteen under master Cleet.

Kinsale, 10 January. 4.40 pm. 'A report has been received that there is a wreck at Courtmacsherry, but there is no confirmation... Kinsale, 13 January. 8.30 am. The General Caulfield, barque, from Newcastle, mistook Courtmacsherry for Cork, struck the bank and became a total wreck. Her cargo of wheat is thoroughly saturated but the crew all saved.'[170]

'The vessel had a cargo of grain (wheat) from South America to England. The crew were saved, but the ship was wrecked. The grain was washed in on the strands. People came from all quarters to gather it, some from thirty miles away... They made shelter for themselves in the caves by the sea, having straw for bed, they were very poor. They remained there until June gathering what the sea had washed in'.[171]

168 *West Cork Eagle & County Advertiser.* 6 April 1878.
169 Ibid. 13 April 1878.
170 B.T. & R.Larn. *Shipwreck Index of Ireland*
171 *Irish Folklore Commission,* schools collection, Kilbrittan 1939.

Collected from Sarah Halnan, old age pensioner of Harbour View, Kilbrittain. She was a witness to the scene. Written by *Máiréad Ní Shúilleabhain* of Rathroon National School. 'The hull and cargo were purchased by a man named O'Driscoll from Courtmacsherry. Up to this time the vessel and cargo were intact. A few days later a terrible storm got up which broke the vessel up and a large quantity of wheat was washed ashore. The purchaser lost all and became bankrupt. The spot where the vessel was wrecked is marked by a buoy at the present day'.[172]

⚓ Fig.27: Courtmacsherry Harbour near a high tide. The sand bar is barely visible under the surface of the water in the middle of the photograph. Many vessels have gone aground and been lost in this vicinity. *Courtesy of Kevin Dwyer.*

172 Ibid.

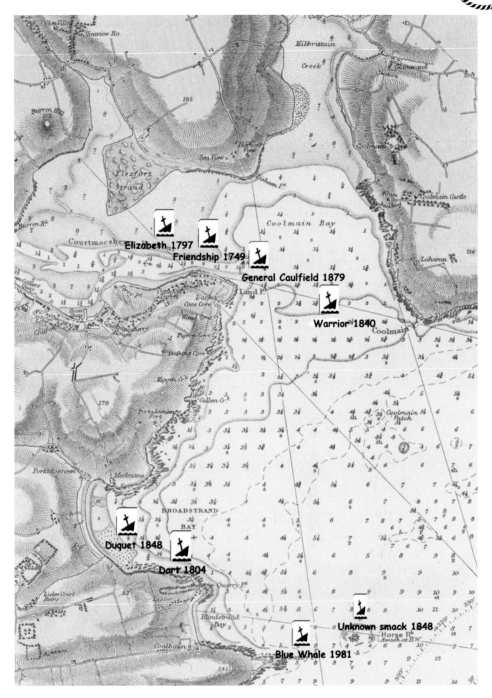

Fig.28: Chart of the Approaches to Courtmacsherry Harbour indicating approximate wreck sites.

Written by Patrick Keohane, Barleyfield, Kilbrittain (pupil) and told to him by James Keohane of the same address.

Robinson Crusoe: Lost at moorings in Kinsale Harbour on 21 May 1880. This 27-ton lugger was run down by the Isle of Man fishing smack at her moorings in Kinsale harbour. The skipper was Corcoran and the vessel carried a crew of eight.[173] There are two listings for this vessel, both identical, but differing in date, one saying 1880 and the other 1881.

Bangalore: This barque was lost 30 miles south-southeast of the Old Head on 6 March 1881.

> Cork, 06 March. 3.10 p.m. 'The Foxhound of London, master Jago, St Malo to Cork with barley, arrived here today having picked up the crew, twelve in number, of the barque Bangalore of Greenock, Liverpool to Port de Galle, master Roberts, whose vessel was abandoned 30 miles south-southeast of the Old Head of Kinsale.'[174]

Glaramara: 12 February 1882.

This steel barque of 678 tons was built in 1877, it carried a crew of 17 and the ship's home port was Whitehaven in the United Kingdom.[175]

⚓ Fig.29: *Glaramara* lost near Frower Point in 1882.
   Source: State Library of South Australia.

173   B.T & R. Larn, *Shipwreck Index of the Irish Coast.*
174   Ibid.
175   B.T & R. Larn. *Shipwreck Index of Ireland.* (Lloyd's Register-Fairplay Ltd, Surrey 2002).

The press report on the event as it appeared in the following day's edition of the *Cork Examiner*:

During Sunday night, when a violent southerly gale was blowing, the barque *Glaramara*, from San Francisco, bound for Queenstown, was forced towards the land, after passing Kinsale Head, and was obliged to drop anchor on a lee shore, off the exposed Oysterhaven. The position of the vessel is a very perilous one, particularly with the southerly gales, but as a powerful tug, the *Mount Etna*, has gone from Queenstown to her assistance, it is hoped she may reach it in time to save the valuable property, as well as the lives of the crew.

Later, 8pm. The tug steamer returned to Queenstown, and brings intelligence of the foundering of the barque referred to above. In addition to her crew there were also aboard the tug- Mr George B Dawson of the firm John Dawson & Company, Mr B. Seaton, and a Kinsale pilot. The latter bought the intelligence first to Queenstown of the ship's danger, having run around in the gale in his pilot cutter. The above gentlemen report that they reached the vessel at 2 pm, she was lying off Oysterhaven and close to the Sovereign Rock. The weather was however, so terrific it was impossible to render any assistance, while endeavouring to near the vessel the tug was struck by a sea that carried away some of the deck houses, and injured her paddle box, several heavy seas breaking on board. At 2 pm, the barque's masts were cut away, and the ship then seemed to ride a little quieter, however at 5 pm, when the people aboard the tug had arranged to lay off for the present, and await a more favourable chance to pass a hawser on board, the *Glaramara* was seen to take a violent plunge-the seas had previously been breaking over her. Those on board the tug partly surmised it was her last dip, as the ship went down to her anchor, as they supposed, with all on board. The tug remained about the vicinity for some time, and then returned to Queenstown. The *Glaramara* was an iron barque of 700 tons, owned in Whitehaven, and had made a splendid run of 116 days to our coast from San Francisco. She was commanded by Captain Morton, and was well known in Queenstown. He was a married man, with four children.

9 pm:-Still later news states that all hands have been saved by the Coastguard's rocket apparatus, and another account that only two of the crew were saved, and those badly injured. Up to the time of writing no really reliable information as to the position of the crew had reached here, and considerable anxiety on this head prevails.
Kinsale, Monday- Information was received at Kinsale yesterday that a large vessel was nearly ashore close by the mouth of the harbour. On proceeding to the scene...I found she was laden with wheat, and on Monday morning about three o'clock while off Kinsale harbour, between Hangman Point and the Sovereign Islands, a terrible breeze being off the land at the time, the crew had to let go two anchors to prevent the vessel from going ashore. She lies in a very dangerous position, being only a few cables length from the shore. As the sea is running very high, it is feared she will draw her anchors and become a total wreck. One of the crew was severely injured on Sunday. He fell off the top mast down on to the deck, and some of his limbs got broken. He was brought ashore yesterday evening by a rocket apparatus, and removed to the workhouse hospital. Slight hopes are entertained of his recovery, as the poor fellow is in a very weak condition.[176]

As announced in our issue yesterday morning, this barque became a total loss at Oysterhaven on Monday evening, but we are glad to say that the uncertainty about the safety of the crew is quite set at rest by their arrival at the Cork Sailors Home yesterday. The remoteness of Oysterhaven and the absence of telegraph communication from that district was the reason why no positive details were obtainable before yesterday. An interview with the crew yesterday enables us to give the following details...No bad weather was experienced during the voyage until Monday 5th, when she was off the western islands. She

176   *Cork Examiner,* 13 February 1883.

then experienced strong gales from the west and south-west accompanied by heavy seas, but got through the storm with the loss of a few sails. From that out the weather was very bad, and a succession of gales, mostly from the points indicated, were encountered, but no other casualty occurred. On Sunday morning at 11 o'clock the land was sighted from the royal yard, and that evening at 5 the Fastnet light being abeam they bore up for the eastward. It was very thick, with a strong southerly gale blowing. At 9 o'clock orders were given to shorten sail, and when one of the crew named Henry Bismark was engaged in this duty (furling the topsails) he was blown off, and fell on the starboard chains on the main deck forehead, a height of 60 feet. Strange to say he escaped with no greater injury than the dislocation of his hip. He was placed below and whatever relief was at hand was afforded. The barque continued her course until two o'clock on Monday morning-it being still very thick- when the orders were given to wear the ship and get sail on her. The land was then in sight, and sail could not be got on her, so orders were given to let the anchors go. The breaking sea was heard all around, but the ship appeared to be in deep water, and holding well. Of course those on board knew nothing of their whereabouts, but when daylight broke they found themselves moored between the Sovereign Rock and Oysterhaven. During the night they burned torches, which caught the attention of the coastguards, and also that of a pilot cutter, which was riding out the gale. In the morning the gale became stronger, with very heavy squalls from the south-west and west, but the barque held well to her anchors until eleven o'clock on Monday morning, when she began to drag. Long before this-just at daybreak-the pilot cutter communicated with Captain Moreton and at his request they went to Queenstown to procure the assistance of a tug, a service which they performed with great celerity, and the coastguards were also observed in readiness on the main land to render assistance with the rocket apparatus in case it were needed. The force of the gale increased, the anchors continued to drag and the barque was driving rapidly on to the shore. The *Mount Etna* was in view about 12 o' clock, but the wind and sea were such that she could not, with regard to her own safety, attempt to render any assistance. Between 2 and 3 o'clock on Monday the force of the gale still increasing with a tremendous sea and the ship still driving ashore, Captain Moreton ordered the masts to be cut away, and at the same time a flag of distress was hoisted to indicate to the coastguards that assistance was needed. They at once brought the rocket apparatus into play, the work of cutting away the masts happening at the same time. The first shot did not reach and the second got foul of the foremast. The fourth line caught the main lower topsail yard, and when the main mast fell, it was secured by one of the apprentices. The removal of the masts eased the barque considerably, but it was evident that she got greatly strained as she leaked freely and all the work at the pumps proved unequal to the task of keeping the water under. The hawser was got from the main land about four o' clock, and as the ship was rapidly sinking, the rescue was proceeded with at once. Captain Moreton ordered that one of the boys should be sent over in the breeches buoy in order to test the cable, and he reached in safety. The next passenger was poor Bismark whose thigh was dislocated. He was placed in the receptacle and was drawn over until he reached within twenty yards of the goal when the hawser snapped, through the ship giving a tremendous lurch, and he fell a depth of ten or twelve feet on rocks, sustaining some severe bruises in addition to the injuries from which he was already suffering. The time became an anxious one then, as the barque was steadily settling down, but the coastguards were very quick in passing over another hawser on the leading line, and as a precaution this time was made so taut. The position of the ship now being far more critical, Captain Moreton ordered that two should go ashore together, the boys being sent first and the seamen afterwards. In this manner all were rescued, Captain Moreton being the last to leave the ship, and he had only just reached the land when she foundered in about six fathoms of water. All on board only escaped with the clothes they wore, and we need hardly say their plight was a wretched one when they reached the land. They were wet as well as cold. However, they received the most generous treatment from Mr Walker, a farmer in the locality. He received all the waifs of the sea into his house, provided them as far as possible with a change of clothes while their own were drying, and in the words of some of the crew, "hospitality is no name for our treatment." Yesterday morning he placed vehicles at their disposal to bring them to the train at Kinsale. The coastguards, the crew desire to say, rendered splendid service, and also helped to minister to the wants of the ship-wrecked mariners. The men arrived in the Cork Sailors Home last evening, and were made very comfortable. Captain Moreton remains at the scene of the wreck. The cargo, we believe was not insured.

In a statement Mr James Logue said-'we got everything ready for the tugboat to unshackle the cable: when it came it could render no assistance, and did not try to render any assistance. He might have towed the ship out when he first came, but did not try; he never came near the ship when we had the signal of distress flying, and he could have saved the men and the ship. It could...if the tug behaved properly they could have taken us away to Queenstown. I consider that they acted very cowardly.

The formation of the coast made the working of the rocket apparatus very difficult. A cliff one hundred feet high faced the vessel, and the hawser had to be so arranged that the men were hauled round to a rock, on to which they were pulled by coastguards stationed below for the purpose. All speak highly of the efficiency of the Coastguard-men.[177]

The rocket apparatus was used to fire a line aboard a vessel in distress close to the shore. The line was secured to a strong point on the vessel and individually the crew were evacuated in a breeches buoy, a circular device with a leg harness attached. The master of the vessel had his certificate suspended for three months owing to having neglected to use the lead line to ascertain the depth.[178] The exact place where the vessel went ashore is not known. However, Larn in his *Shipwreck Index of Ireland* states that it is near Prehane, and Mick O'Rourke of www.Irishshipwrecks.com concludes that it is Frower Point, a distance of 0.65m from one point to the other.

⚓ Fig.30: The Glaramara went ashore somewhere in the area between Frower and Prehane Point as indicated by the white arrows. The red star at Cummeraduna marks the area where some shipwreck debris was recently discovered. *Courtesy of Kevin Dwyer.*

177 *Cork Examiner.* 14 February 1883.
178 www.Irishshipwrecks.com

Charles: Lost twelve miles south-southeast of the Old Head, 30 June 1885. This 46-ton barge (one of three) under sail was en route from Rochester to Tralee in wind conditions force 9 when she foundered. The two other barges, *George* (44 tons) and *Abeona* (42 tons) were all being towed by a tug which rescued the combined crews of six men.[179]

Mary: A 576-ton Norwegian barque collided with a Liverpool vessel and sank 50 miles south of the Old Head on 7 February 1886.[180]

Ida: Wrecked at the Old Head on 1 August 1886. A schooner of 74 tons carrying a cargo of coal on a voyage from Runcorn to Glin. The vessel was owned by Tyrrell of Arklow and carried a crew of four.[181]

A lighter: These were barges that were used to lighten vessels.

> On the 12th June 1888 the harbourmaster was informed on Friday last that a lighter belonging to Patrick Sheehan had sunk in the navigable part of the Western bridge. On Saturday morning the masters of three vessels were told they would not be allowed to pass through as the bridge-man did not consider it safe to do so. Soundings were taken around and over the sunken craft and found that vessels could pass with safety on a rising tide. By permission Sheehan got the harbour commissioners lighter up there on Sunday. Yesterday I went up with our boat and some ropes and grappled, succeeding in lifting and bringing her ashore on the beach, leaving the bridge free as before. The Harbourmaster was directed to caution Sheehan.
> Written up by Joseph Thuillier, chairman.[182]

Comrade: An unregistered Manx fishing boat of 40 tons was fishing out of Kinsale when she was struck by heavy seas in a bad gale. The boat was damaged and was partially wrecked. One crewman was lost 14 miles off the Old Head on 2 May 1888.[183]

Nicholas Mullaney: Stranded and lost in a southwesterly force 6 in Bullen's Bay on 24 June 1890. A smack of 30 tons on a run from Cork to Rosscarbery, it was carrying a cargo of maize under E. Collins and a crew of two. The vessel was owned by M. Ahern of Youghal.[184]

Another report gives the following details. The vessel was 29 tons, official number 14329 and built at Ballinacurra, near Midleton. Her cargo consisted of 49.5 tons of maize worth £350, which was consigned for Thomas Shorten, Rosscarbery, from Hall and Co of Cork. The following is a statement given by the master of the vessel, Edward Collins of 5 Hillgrove Lane, Cork:

> We put into Kinsale Harbour wind-bound on 21st and left on the 23rd for Rosscarbery, and when we got as far as the Seven Heads, we put back for Kinsale Harbour owing to strong head winds and a nasty cross sea. The said ship was running for Kinsale Harbour under mainsail, staysail and jib, and when about half a mile off Old Head of Kinsale, we thought we saw the Old Head light, but we were not sure. The light bore about northwest. We altered our course from east-southeast to north-northeast in order to make Kinsale.

179   B.T. & R. Larn. *Shipwreck Index of Ireland.*
180   *Historic Shipwrecks of the East & West Cork Coast.*
181   B.T & R. Larn, *Shipwreck Index of Ireland.*
182   *Minute Book,* Kinsale Harbour Commissioners from November 1870- July 1890.
183   *Historic Shipwrecks of the East & West Cork Coast.*
184   B.T. & R. Larn, *Shipwreck Index of Ireland.*

In jibing the mainsail the lacing gave way and we lowered the gaff to leave a new lacing, and during the time we were doing so and hoisting the gaff, I could not properly attend to the helm. The weather was so thick that we could not see the land and before we got the mainsail properly hoisted we grounded on a reef of rocks in Bullen's Bay. As soon as the vessel struck we lowered the sails and tried the pumps and found she was making no water. As the vessel went on the rocks at high water and as she was then making no water, we remained by her until next morning and about 6 a.m., we found she was making a good deal of water and we could not keep her clear with the pump. We had one compass on board, but no chart or lead line. After pounding, she developed a leak and there was about four foot of water in the hold. The vessel appears to have received considerable damage and is likely to become a total wreck. When the vessel struck the sea was smooth with a ground swell from the southeast and being under the lee of the land the wind was light. The vessel was not going more than one mile an hour when she struck. The Coast Guard offered assistance about 3 a.m., on the 25th which I declined and at 6 a.m., I signalled for assistance when an anchor was laid out and the pump kept going. The Coast Guard took ashore all our sails and loose gear.[185]

Fishing Vessel and Crew Lost off Kinsale: 15 October 1891.

On the afternoon of Thursday, 15 October 1891, a fishing yawl owned by James Carroll, a local fish merchant, departed for the local fishing grounds southeast of the mouth of the harbour. They shot their nets about six miles east of the Old Head and proceeded to drift for the coming night.

At about 6pm a strong breeze from the southeast arose and later developed into a strong gale. Many vessels hauled their nets early and ran for port. Patrick Kerrigan, the skipper of the vessel, sensing the danger that was imminent, set about the task of hauling the gear (drift nets) aboard. The conditions had deteriorated considerably before all the gear was aboard and the crew were thrown into the water with no chance of being rescued. This was further complicated by the darkness that prevailed on that particular night. Nothing more was heard or seen until the following evening when oars bearing the name of the vessel's owner and other items were picked up by a man named Manning near the Old Head. This event cast a shadow of gloom over the town, and the shops were closed as a mark of respect.

The vessel carried a crew of four including the skipper. The skipper's son Denis was also on board, as was Michael Regan and a young man named Cotter. Michael Regan's loss was especially poignant as he had also recently lost his two sons at sea. He was survived by his wife and one daughter. The skipper lost his father to the sea some years prior to this and was survived by his wife and one daughter to mourn his loss. Cotter was survived by both his parents.[186]

---

185 Depositions. *Register of Examinations on Oath concerning Wrecks and Casualties on the Coasts of the United Kingdom,* by the Receiver of Wrecks for the District of Kinsale, 448th section of the Merchant Shipping Act 1884, marine Department Committee.
186 *Cork Examiner,* 17 October *1891.*

On Saturday, 3 November, Thomas F. Brady of 11 Percy Place, Dublin, writing in 'Letters to the Editor' in that day's *Cork Examiner*, reported the following.

'Immediately on my reporting the matter to the Shipwrecked Fishermen and Mariners Society they in their most generous manner sent me £5 for immediate help. I have also received £2 from a lady. For their timely donations I am gratefully thankful'.

The following extract a month later in Letters to the Editor appears as follows:

Dear Sir- Kindly permit me to acknowledge through your column the following contributions received by me since the publication of my last list in aid of the widows and orphans of the four fishermen who were drowned off Kinsale Head, County Cork on the 14th October. The directors of the Munster and Leinster Bank and F C T Gascolgne £3 each; Alfred Rowling and VN, £2.2s each; NC, Dublin and Anonymous,£2 each; Dr Paton, Thomas Crosbie, Miss Mc Kinley, F E Curry, Mrs Keane and JM,£1 each;Cornelius Mc Loughlin and Col Sweet, £1.1s each. Arthur Nugent, Miss Glifie and RG Callanan, 10s each; D Condon, 5s and E Harvey, 2s 6d. For these generous contributions I feel deeply grateful.

These four poor fellows were out fishing off Kinsale Head on the 14th October, when one of those violent storms which lately   visited our coast suddenly arose and left them struggling to reach the harbour. Their boat was picked up the next day, keel uppermost...... It is proposed to purchase a small annuity for them, say for ten years and thus keep them from the poorhouse. Towards this end I have already received £54. The smallest contribution will thankfully be received and may be lodged to the Munster and Leinster Bank to the credit of the "Kinsale Fishing Disaster Fund" or sent to Very Rev Cannon Cotter, Kinsale, Lieut Colonel Daly, JP, Kinsale or Francis Walker, ESQ. Manager Munster and Leinster Bank Kinsale, or to me-Yours truly

Thomas F Brady,
16 Percy Place.
Dublin.[187]

Guelph: 12 November 1891

The ship was originally built in Quebec in 1839 for the transatlantic trade under the name *Independence*. Her first owner was John Dunn of Belfast. In her later years she carried timber from eastern Canada to Europe.

In August 1888, twelve of her crew abandoned her in the western Atlantic, after hoisting messages of distress that attracted the *Persian Monarch* steamship. Landing in New York, the crew alleged that the captain and two mates who remained on board had bored holes in her hull in an attempt to scuttle her for insurance claim purposes. The captain and mate were convicted of fraud and given a sentence of ten years penal servitude. In a further incident, in April 1890, when starting a passage to Quebec under ballast, the tow rope parted and she collided with the quay wall at Greenock, inflicting significant damage to the hull.

187 *Cork Examiner* 19 November *1891.*

On the evening of Thursday 12 November during a southerly gale of at least force nine in Courtmacsherry Bay, she grounded and was lost, with a loss of eight lives from a crew of twelve. En route to Liverpool, she had become waterlogged during the gales and with tar barrels burning to show her distress, approached the coast so closely that the coastguards tried to warn her off. But it was clear to Captain Santerre that his vessel was breaking up fast and he urged as many of his crew as possible to join him in staying with the forward deckhouse that was becoming detached from the vessel. Those that did survived with just one exception. Of the eight that died, most were probably killed by portions of the timber cargo that were strewn around the water close to the vessel. Three bodies were washed ashore, at which stage those still unaccounted for were listed as the mate Jones, a Swede named Olsen, carpenter James McNeill and two others. The wreckage survivors and bodies were washed ashore on the White Strand.[188]

Newspaper accounts for the time constantly refer to Garretstown as the point where the wreckage and bodies were washed ashore. However, local tradition has always pointed to the White Strand. The late Ted Manning, who lived at the north side of the White Strand, always referred to the *Guelph* as coming in on the White Strand (his father would have witnessed this event). This is also confirmed by research@ shipwrecks.uk.com. There has also always been a tendency with some reporters to collectively call the two beaches the same name, Garretstown. It is difficult to ascertain where exactly the vessel hit the bottom; the Barrels, a reef in the middle of the bay, is often mentioned. However, if this were the case, it would be very difficult to envisage the vessel having any survivors at all. It would also mean that the wreckage would have mostly ended up on the northern shore of the bay in a near storm force southerly wind. Given the distance (nearly 2 miles) between the Barrels and Garretstown/Garrylucas area, it would be inconceivable that there would have been any survivors. The area of the White Strand where most of the bodies were washed up is a very shallow area with several reefs, most notably the area between *Droichead Muscán* and *Droichead na Fian*, where a huge long wave breaks in bad weather conditions about 200 yards off the beach from the low-water mark. This is likely to be the area she grounded in. The area off Garretstown strand is by contrast sandy bottomed with no reefs immediately off the beach. Later reports confirm (when the light keeper at the Old Head stated she was wrecked inside the *Muscán* reef and later sunk a half mile from the shore).[189]

The first reports to hit the press came on Saturday, 14 November, two days after the disaster.

The coastguards at Courtmacsherry observed a ship making distress signals to the north of the Old Head. It was blowing a gale from the south-south-west. The officer in charge prepared the rocket cart in readiness for a certain tragedy. They headed for the Broad Strand where it was initially thought the ship might end up. On arrival at the Broad Strand there was no light to be seen and after a period of time the rocket crew returned to Courtmacsherry. They presumed she grounded somewhere in the bay. At this juncture the *Guelph*, taking advantage of a temporary lull in the wind, tacked out to sea, and she succeeded for a while in keeping a good distance off the shore. But when the wind again picked up she was blown shore wards. It being impossible to weather the Old Head, an

188 Research@shipwrecks.uk.com
189 *Historic Shipwrecks of the East & West Cork Coast*, Dúchas: The Heritage Service, 2000.

attempt was made to anchor; however she dragged until she struck the reef outside the strand, and soon filled with water. About 3am a huge sea covered the vessel which it broke up in pieces. The captain and the other survivors lashed themselves to the deckhouse and were washed ashore after having narrowly missing protruding rocks. Shortly before midnight a rider was dispatched from Garretstown and arrived in Courtmacsherry at 1am, and requisitioned the services of the lifeboat. The ship had been driven ashore at Garretstown (probably the White Strand) and the local rocket crew had failed to get a line aboard the stricken ship which was fast breaking up. The big gun was fired and the lifeboat crew assembled; however, many of the lifeboat crew refused to venture out into the bay, given the horrendous conditions that morning. Some of the coastguards threw in their lot with the remaining lifeboat crew and the vessel departed. As soon as daylight appeared the lifeboat visited the scene of the wreck but to no avail, as the ship had long gone to pieces. The lifeboat returned to Courtmacsherry that morning at 9am.

On Friday morning, 13 November two of the bodies from the ill-fated vessel were washed ashore. They were very disfigured having been dashed off the jagged rocks before being reaching land. Large quantities of wreckage continued to be washed up on the strand and armed coastguards kept watch over this. On Saturday 14 November a large number of people visited the scene of the wreck; not a timber from the ship remained on the scene, testimony to the fury of the sea and a change in wind direction. None of the missing bodies had been recovered that day, and it was thought that they had been taken seaward, given that the wind had backed to the north-east since the morning of the disaster. Several boats with crews numbering six to ten were in the vicinity of the wreck site with a view to salvaging the baulks of timber that remained in the water, and which comprised the cargo of the now-wrecked vessel. Some were successful in their efforts, and a large store of baulks had been put ashore south of Barry's Point pending sale by the Customs authorities. Many boats had secured several pieces; however, when taking them in tow and running into the tide and weather, they had lost many of them. One such boat had five large timbers, but when they came to the vicinity of the Horse Rock the strong ebb tide took them out to sea. The whole bay was a mass of floating timber and the strong wind from the north-east took much of it away to sea. Much anxiety prevailed in Courtmacsherry as to the safety of local vessels *Harry Herbert*, *Captain Murray* and *Gwain Maid*. These craft had sailed in ballast a few days before the disaster and encountered the full fury of the weather. However, a telegram had arrived that day stating that all were safe and docked in Newport, South Wales. The weather they encountered was the worst they had ever witnessed.[190]

Monday and Tuesday saw three more bodies given up by the sea and more debris from the wreck washed on to the strand. A Queenstown insurance agent Mr Scott visited the scene and had a large number of men employed gathering baulks from the cargo and storing them safely for auction. The captain of the *Guelph*, a French-Canadian by the name of Andrew Avelin Santerre and the four remaining survivors were still in the neighbourhood, having been put up and hospitably treated by the local fishermen. In his account the captain stated that on Thursday morning when he was passing the Galley Head the wind changed from south-southwest to south and increased in force until it reached the fury of a hurricane. The foresails and topsails were torn to shreds and the vessel became very difficult to manoeuvre. Towards evening the wind increased its strength and tore the remaining sails to tatters. Several attempts were made to rig temporary sails in order to clear the Old Head, alas this also failed and the vessel was rapidly making way towards the fatal stormbound shore. They had been making distress signals for some time, and when the ship struck the reef at 9pm it broke up rapidly. Three rockets were fired by the Old Head coastguard team which was three quarters of a mile distant on the shore. Two fell wide of the mark, and the last one landed on the deck. The crew were at this point clinging to the rigging and unable to get to the rescue line, and the ship was completely broken up. The captain and some members of the crew held to the fore deckhouse which had become detached from the deck; one crewman was washed off this and drowned. Three others were thrown into the water after the deckhouse hit a rock. Fortunately for them there were lots of beams in the water, and they clung on to these. Meanwhile, the captain and an Irishman by the name of Pat Molloy were still on the deckhouse which was washed off the rock. At this point they were 100 yards from shore when Molloy fell off and the captain with one hand on the victim and one on the deckhouse managed to hang on until they beached on the sandy shore. Here they were pulled from the surf by some of the large crowd which had congregated on the shore. The plank with the three other survivors came in immediately after, and the exhausted men were rescued by the onlookers. The survivors' names (in addition to the captain and Molloy) were Thomas Ryan, Barney McLevy (Newry,) both Irishmen, and a Welshman named David Hughes. The names of only five of the men who were drowned were known to the captain or the surviving members of the crew. Two of them aged about 18 were from Limerick, one being known as 'Tom'. The carpenter was a Swede, the mate a Welshman named Jones, MacLoughlin a Dublin man, Robensen a Frenchman, Olsen, also a Swede, and James MacNeill from the north of Ireland. The bodies that were recovered were those of Robensen, MacLoughlin and one of the Limerick men. The coastguards and the police from Ballinspittle kept a constant vigil over the washed-up cargo and at one stage a policeman was forced to let off a shot to deter a raider during the night. Molloy spoke very highly of captain Santerre, who risked his own life to save his. Sergeant Fleming, RIC, of Ballinspittle on examining the pockets of the drowned Frenchman Robensen, took a bundle of papers which he handed to Patrick O'Connell, publican. The latter having dried the papers to examine them found a sum of £35 and a bank deposit receipt for a further £35 all of which was obtained by the Frenchman's surviving friends. Another incident relates to Joanne Forde of Garrylucas who rushed into the oncoming waves to save a sailor struggling for his life in the foam. This near-dead man was bought to Timothy Downey's house nearby where he was put into a warm bed and soon revived. Mrs Healy and her son John and other son (unnamed) were also accorded great credit for the treatment they gave to some of the survivors in their home.[191]

In the aftermath of the tragedy there were repercussions for some members of the lifeboat crew. An enquiry was held as to why some members of the crew refused to go to sea on the fateful night. After going into all the circumstances of the case, the second coxswain Mr T. Collins was called upon to hand in his resignation, and several others had their names struck off the lifeboat crew list. Other incidents relating to the event occurred in the week following the Thursday night catastrophe. On the night of Wednesday 18 November a conflict between the coastguards and civilians over recovered baulks of timber occurred at Lislee. Some timber had been bought ashore at Broad Strand by local fishermen, and handed over to the coastguard. He received information that the timber was going to be the subject of a raid that night. They saw two carts at Lislee that night and challenged the occupants, a scuffle ensued and the coastguards were disarmed and beat a retreat. A man from Timoleague by the name of John Tobin, a carpenter was later arrested and charged with being one of the attacking parties.[192]

The Honorary secretary (Courtmacsherry Lifeboat), Mr Townshend, in his report, remarked that the lack of a telegraph station in Courtmacsherry had resulted in undue delay in getting word to the lifeboat, as the Old Head Coastguard Station was 14 miles away by horseback.[193]

191   *Cork Examiner,* 18 November 1891.
192   *Cork Examiner,* 20 November 1891.
193   M. Hurley. *Home from the Sea,* the story of Courtmacsherry Lifeboat 1825-1995. Colour Books Ltd 1995, p.18.

City of Chicago: 1 July 1892

The *City of Chicago* is one of the better known ships that came to grief on the western side of the Old Head of Kinsale. The photographic record that is preserved has helped to keep it alive today in the minds of the people in that area. The site is a popular haunt for anglers and commercial fishermen who hunt the prolific pollock shoals around the wreck site. The sometimes rusty coloured lobster reminds one of what lurks among the remaining debris. It is also a popular dive site. The location of the wreck is found on the point of a headland known as *Rinn a'Gortín*. The cleft where the wreck lodged is known as *Poll na Bolg*. This headland marks the southern most point of Holeopen Bay West.

⚓ Fig.31: *City of Chicago*　　*Source : Clydesite.uk*

During dense fog the *City of Chicago* went ashore at a headland about a half a mile north-north-west of the Old Head lighthouse on 1 July 1892. The ship was owned by the Inman and International Steamship Company and was on a voyage from New York to Liverpool, and had on board 350 passengers and 155 crew. The ship was a four-masted steamer of 3364 tons and was built by C.O'Connell of Glasgow in 1883.
The early part of the voyage is best described by General Mc Ateer of the US army who was a saloon passenger on the steamship.

"We left New York on Wednesday afternoon, June 22nd for Queenstown and Liverpool, having 130 saloon, 138 second cabin, and 92 steerage passengers aboard, also 21 bags of mail and a general cargo consisting principally of wheat, bacon and dead meat etc. The weather for the greater part of the voyage was excellent...The only incident of the voyage up to the time we were stranded was the passing in mid ocean of a large derelict ship with one mast standing on which were set a number of sails. The bow of the craft seemed intact , but the stern was all battered, in leading to the supposition that she had been in a collision...On Friday at 4.45pm we were abreast of the Fastnet Signal Station to which we signalled our name, and were then in hope of meeting the Queenstown tender at about 9pm. At 5.30pm the weather suddenly became thick, but lifted at intervals. I was on the promenade deck at five minutes to 8pm...I felt the ship strike something hard and at the same moment the man on lookout shouted "breakers ahead". He had scarcely said so when the ship crashed with terrific force upon the rocks.[194]

The initial telegram from Lloyd's Signal Station at the Old Head of Kinsale, dated 1 July, 9.17am, states:

"The steamer *City of Chicago* is ashore about two miles west of this station"

A further telegram from the same station at 9.32pm, states:

"The Steamer *City of Chicago* ashore half a mile inside of the head; stem into the cliff; launching her boats. Life-saving apparatus coming. Sea moderate and smooth. Wind S.S.W., light, and dense fog".

A telegram from Queenstown at 11pm, states:

"Old Head of Kinsale wires that the Inman Steamer *City of Chicago*, from New York for Liverpool, via Queenstown is ashore a half a mile west of the head in a dense fog. Tugs have been dispatched.[195]

The agents for the shipping line, the Cummins brothers, dispatched three tugs to the scene. Other vessels that assisted at the scene included two vessels from the Clyde shipping company, also based in Queenstown. The *Stormcock*, a powerful tug from Liverpool, also came to the scene from the aforementioned port. The vessel struck the rocks about a half an hour before high water, so that the chances of floating her were doubtful. The fore compartment of the ship was filled with water.[196]

Others were taken off by the vessels on stand-by and brought to Queenstown. The *Irish Times* reported favourably on the help the stricken passengers received from the local rescue services and the people of the area. Over 200 people were evacuated by lifesaving ladders suspended from the top of the steep hillside. The crew then laid planks from the starboard bow onto the rockface to aid the passengers. At the top they were taken by local farmers to the coastguard station and were very kindly treated. The vessel carried 20 bags of mail; this along with the luggage was transported by the attendant vessels to Queenstown. The majority of the passengers were dispatched from

194   *Irish Times*. 4 July 1892.
195   *West Cork Eagle & County Advertiser*, 2 July 1892.
196   *Ibid*.

Queenstown to Dublin and from there to their various destinations. This was paid for by the shipping company.

A telegram to Reuters on Tuesday 1 July, at 3.30pm, contained the following information on the matter:

> It is now just past the tide on which it was hoped to float the *City of Chicago*. No effort could possibly be made to get the vessel off, owing to a break in the weather. Last night a fresh breeze from the south-west sprung up and continues. This caused a heavy roll from the Atlantic in that exposed headland and made the vessel list to a more dangerous position. She is now broadside to the shore, the hull being still further injured. The commander and the crew, however, remain on board. A considerable portion of the cargo has been transferred to the steamers in attendance and a Liverpool tug laden with a good part of the fresh beef proceeded for Milford Haven. During the night the work of transhipping the cargo had to be abandoned and attempts this morning have not been successful. It is now feared that the fate of the vessel is sealed, and that any effort to float would be attended with the gravest danger of the vessel foundering in deep water.[197]

⚓ Fig.32; Debris from the *City of Chicago* wreck site. *Courtesy of John Collins.*

197　*Irish Times.* 6 July 1892.

⚓ Fig.33: More debris from the *City of Chicago*. Courtesy of John Collins.

⚓ Fig.34: Plate from the *City of Chicago*. *Author's Collection*.

⚓ Fig.35: *City of Chicago* on the rocks at *Rinn a' Gortín*, 1892. *Author's Collection.*

The *Irish Times* had a further update on its Friday 4 July edition. It reported that the wind freshened that night and by morning the ship had broken in two, parting amidships. The forward portion was wedged into the recess on the shore and the aft part hung precariously over deeper water (about 8 fathoms). On Thursday, the crew were landed in Queenstown by the tug *Kingfisher* and proceeded for Liverpool via Dublin and Holyhead.

Captain Redford, who had made 160 previous crossings, was suspended for nine months for proceeding too fast in fog and not checking his depth with the lead-line.[198]

A few artefacts in the form of dinner plates from the vessel are still to be seen today in some houses in the surrounding area. An interesting element of the story is the sighting of an abandoned vessel in the mid Atlantic. According to local lore, it was always believed that, prior to a vessel being lost at sea, a phantom ship was sighted with her tattered sails. In the southwest of Ireland this was known as the *Arthrach Mhaol*. This is recalled by the late Jeremiah Keohane in a local school folklore collection:

> About fifty years ago when tales of phantom ships were rife in the locality, a ship was seen to come into the strand opposite *Tobar an Each*. She appeared to be a three masted barque. Two men Dan Hayes and Séan Ó Cuinn who perceived her from the cliff top raced

198   Edward J. Bourke. *Shipwrecks of the Irish Coast 1105-1993*. P.115.

for the coastguard station, to report that a vessel was in grave danger of becoming a wreck on the rocks near *Tobar an Each*. The lifesaving apparatus was brought to the scene but it was a labour in vain. When they arrived they saw the vessel sailing gracefully over the rocks and away around the lighthouse. The onlookers were dumbfounded at the amazing spectacle. Two of the crew followed on around the cliff-top. They saw her steer for *Cuairt a Purtín* where she disappeared. They came to the conclusion that she was one of the phantom ships[199]

Fig.36: Chest and stand from the *City of Chicago*.

199   *Irish Folklore Commission*. Schools collection. Old Head N.S. 1939.

Capri: A yacht of 11 tons owned by Henry Villiers Stuart of the Royal Cork Yacht Club. Miss-stayed and grounded in Upper Cove, Kinsale, on 10 September 1892.[200]

Kelburne: Stranded and lost at the east side of the Old Head on 26 March 1893. A 200-ton vessel that was out of Cork for Schull with general cargo went ashore in calm conditions.[201]

This steam vessel was built of steel and carried a cargo of 135 tons of flour. In very thick fog (poor visibility), on 26 Sunday, she grounded abreast of the Bream Rock, a short distance north of the Old Head lighthouse on the east side. Her bow was barely above water and the remainder of the vessel submerged, according to the deposition of the master Robert Ross.[202]

⚓   Fig.37: The east side of the Old Head showing the Bream Rock, where the *Kelburne* was lost in 1893, marked by a green star. The *Ardent* 1984 in the foreground indicated by the red star. The *Adelaide*, 1862, indicated by the yellow star and the *Sally Brown* 1963, purple star were all lost here. The white diamond on the left marks the spot named *Leaba Loinge* and the white diamond on the right is in *Cuas Cannon*/Gunhole, where there is archaeological evidence to suggest a gun ship foundered at this inlet.   *Courtesy of Kevin Dwyer.*

Foam: A 58-ton yacht Lloyds Class A1, with nine hands and four passengers left Summercove, "also known as Upper Cove", on 19 August 1893, bound for Dartmouth. The yacht miss-stayed and went ashore under Charles Fort in a fresh breeze from the south-southwest. The owner of the vessel was Marmaduke Cramer and assistance was given by the local coastguard. Recorded by the Receiver of Wrecks, J. Regan.[203]

---

200 Deposition, *Register of Examinations on Oath concerning Wrecks and Casualties on the Coasts of the United Kingdom.*
201 B.T & R. Larn, *Shipwreck Index of Ireland.*
202 Deposition, *Register of Examinations on Oath concerning Wrecks and Casualties on the Coasts of the United Kingdom.*
203 Ibid.

Courcies: A 54-ton registered Milford Haven dandy, official number 98396, went on the shore in Upper Cove, Kinsale on the 28 December 1893. The weather was fine with a light breeze and it was hoped that by lightening the vessel she would come off on the next tide. In the opinion of a custom house inquest, a proper lookout was not kept for the navigation buoys.[204]

Gerda: A 15- ton brig was lost following a collision in wind conditions northwest force 5 off the Old Head, 15 July 1895.[205]

Petrel: A pilot schooner of 82 tons was lost at Black Head on 26 February 1897. She had come from Kinsale seeking pilotage.[206]

The vessel was built in Cork in 1848 and left Kinsale on a flood tide in a south west gale. The following evidence was given by John Williams, a crew member of the vessel.

> We boarded two pilots in thick weather with a misty rain at 12.30 noontime. The vessel was under closed reef canvas, trying to make the land. The lookout saw nothing to indicate shore, and later saw breakers on the weather bow. I saw the captain put the helm hard up, the vessel does not bear very quickly, but she cleared the breakers, we saw nothing else and I thought we were clear of all. But in less than five minutes she struck another rock and came up all standing. The captain ordered sails lowered, but although this was immediately done she still remained fixed and started to roll heavily. We did all possible to get her off, to no effect. We heard her commencing to break up, we got into our boat and finding afterwards that there was about three feet of water above the cabin floor and we gave up and came ashore.

Further evidence was given by Michael Leahy:

> The coastguard boat came alongside offered assistance and advised us to leave. Since the tide left we have examined the vessel and find the deck is breaking up, main mast sunk, her stern in deep water, the rock evidently through her bottom and no possible chance of saving the vessel.[207]

The receiver of wrecks, T. Banks, was witness to these statements given at the Old Head on 28 February 1897. Some days after the event, a group of men from the Old Head got on the wrong side of the law when they visited Kinsale:

> Information was received at the Kinsale Police Barrack yesterday that some men belonging to Courceys country were in the town during the morning, and trying to dispose of the sale of some spars, rigging, and sails, belonging to the ill-fated pilot boat the Petrel, of Cork Harbour, which was lost on Friday last during a fog at the Old Head. Acting on the information, Sargent Gettings and some other constables proceeded to the World's End, and took into custody five men belonging to the Old Head, Florence Mahony (2), Edward Fitzgerald, Laurence Sullivan, and John Mahony. They had the goods complained of in their possession in a yawl, and it appears that they failed in selling them, and hearing the police got information of the fact, they were about to take the goods to the Custom House, so as

204   Ibid.
205   B.T & R.Larn, *Shipwreck Index of Ireland.*
206   E.J. Bourke *Shipwrecks of the Irish Coast 1105-1993*, p. 113.
207   Deposition, *Register of Examinations on Oath concerning Wrecks and Casualties on the Coasts of the United Kingdom.*

to palliate the offence. When taken into custody they said they got the goods from the owner. They were then charged with the larceny, and brought before Captain Perry at the Police Barracks, where after an investigation being held, they were discharged to appear at the Kinsale Petty Sessions on Saturday, the goods in the meantime being retained in the possession of the Custom house authority.[208]

There were two Old Head men named Florence O'Mahony, one was known as Flor *Mór,* the other as Flor *Beag.*

Henry Thuillier: A 28-ton dandy broke from her moorings at Kinsale and wrecked on the shore in October 1898.[209] The records held at the Dublin Customs House state that she was lost at the Lobster Quay.

Mary Ann: Was lost six miles southeast of the Old Head when she collided with the steamship *Rockabill.* Four of the eight crew were lost, date and year unknown.[210]

Marion: Lost while fishing in an east-southeast force 9 on 1 October 1898. A lugger of 6 tons, owned by Mrs. Robinson of Kinsale. She carried a crew of four and the skipper was P. Owen.[211]

Shamrock: A small lugger lost off the Blockhouse in Kinsale Harbour, following a collision with a fishing dandy the *Stella* on 9 September 1899.[212]

208   *Cork Examiner.* 3 March 1997. p. 5.
209   B.T & R. Larn, *Shipwreck Index of Ireland.*
210   *Historic Shipwrecks of the East & West Cork Coast.*
211   B.T & R. Larn, *Shipwreck Index of Ireland.*
212   Ibid.

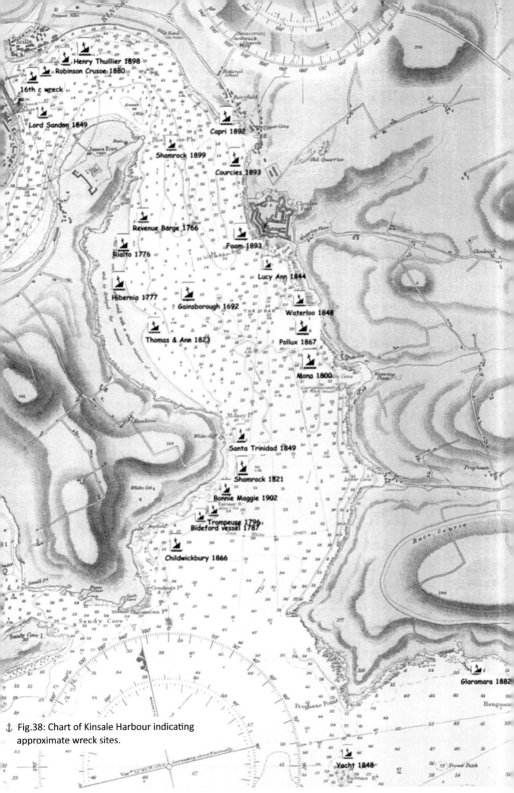

Henry Thuillier 1898

Robinson Crusoe 1880

16th c wreck

Lord Sandon 1849

Capri 1892

Shamrock 1899

Courcies 1893

Revenue Barge 1766

Foam 1893

Rialto 1776

Lucy Ann 1844

Hibernia 1777

Gainsborough 1692

Waterloo 1848

Thomas & Ann 1823

Pollux 1867

Mona 1800

Santa Trinidad 1849

Shamrock 1821

Bonnie Maggie 1902

Trompeuse 1796
Bideford vessel 1787

Childwickbury 1866

Glaramara 1882

Fig.38: Chart of Kinsale Harbour indicating
approximate wreck sites.

Yacht 1848

Chapter V: 1901-1926

Bonnie Maggie: This fishing vessel of Kinsale came to grief on Thursday evening, 6 March 1902 at the entrance to Kinsale Harbour. The hooker returning from the fishing grounds in dense fog struck the Farmer Rock immediately south of Money Point and about one cable from the shore. She sustained serious damage and half filled with water whilst lying on top of the rock. The rock is only barely covered at high water and the crew's fear that it would not come off was justified. The following day, Friday, its fishing gear was removed and nothing could be done to extricate her from her perilous position. The *Bonnie Maggie* was owned by R. A. Williams, who had shortly before refurbished her and installed a new boiler. The Farmer Rock is a dangerous hazard for shipping entering the harbour and this was frequently brought to the attention of the Harbour Board with a view to having a perch erected on it.[213]

Euterpe: A four-masted German barque of 2,129 tons was lost on 8 September 1902 at position 50 32.35′N　08 31.11′W. The vessel was on a voyage from Port Talbot to Pisagua (Chile) with a cargo of 3159 tons of stone coal, when it exploded, leading to the loss of six crewmen. The explosion was possibly caused by coal dust.[214]

Driving Mist: Lost off the Old Head in storm force conditions on 17 November 1902. This 79-ton ketch with a cargo of coal was bound from Lydney (UK) to Kilbrittain with a crew of four under Captain Scilly. All hands were saved despite adverse weather conditions, the wind blowing up to storm force 10 from the south-southeast.[215]

This vessel was probably due to land at Burren Pier.

Alpha: This 19-ton Manx fishing lugger was lost about four miles south-southwest of the Old Head after colliding with the Cork registered dandy *Red Knight*, on 22 October 1903.[216]
Approximate position 51.31.00 N 08.32.00 W

213　*Cork Examiner,* 10 March 1902.
214　www.wrecksite.eu
215　B.T & R. Larn. *Shipwreck Index of the Irish Coast*, (Lloyd's Register-Fairplay Ltd) 2002.
216　Ibid.

Faulconnier: 1 January 1904.

The 1,708-ton French barque from St Nazaire left San Francisco with a cargo of barley for Queenstown on 4 August, 1903. The vessel had an uneventful passage and was nearing her final destination when a strong easterly wind developed. It was a very dark night with poor visibility and at approximately 6pm a squall developed. The ship had at this time lost her bearings when about 3 miles off the land. They may have mistaken the bay of Courtmacsherry for Queenstown and changed tack.[217]
The vessel soon afterwards hit the Crook Rock in *Cuas na Géime*, a short distance east of Travara on the southeast corner of the Seven Heads.[218]

The vessel was firmly held and when the crew were leaving her there was upwards of four feet of water on the deck and the prospect of the ship being salvaged had gone. With the assistance of local fishermen, the 26 man crew were saved and conveyed to Courtmacsherry. The crew were looked after by the French Consul, Mr. J.W. Scott. A local tug, the *Flying Sportsman*, went to evaluate the situation but could not render any help to the stricken vessel, which was wedged on the rock and facing in a north-east direction. It was thought that the cargo of barley would swell quickly and this would contribute to the decks bursting.[219]

According to UK Hydrographic office, the wreck lies in an east-west position with the bow facing east in a general depth of 2.5 to 6 fathoms. It is in a very broken-up state, with main spars and metal plates visible and covered with kelp. Part of the steering gear rises vertically near the west end to a height of approximately 8ft. They give the exact position of 51. 34. 63N and 08.42.04W. This location is at odds with the opinion of local diver Chris Guy and historian Michael Madden, who place the location around the corner to the west from this.

Inverkip: This steel barque was lost 55 miles south of the Old Head on 13 August 1904. This 1,354-ton vessel carrying a cargo of wheat collided with the Glasgow registered barque *Loch Carron*: twenty of the twenty two crew were lost.[220]

Monarch: A steam trawler of 65 tons was lost 20 miles south of the Old Head on 13 October 1907.[221]

Rob Roy: Official number 38748 was a 93-ton schooner owned by Richard Farrell of Youghal and was built in 1886. She carried a crew of five and on 23 December 1907. She left Cardiff in fine weather, bound for Youghal with a cargo of 159 tons of coal and other goods. Later on the following day, around midnight, they sighted a dim light and thought it to be Roche's Point. However, it was the Old Head light (only dim lit about 7 days, the light sequence changed about this time) in poor conditions, the wind

217 *Cork Examiner.* 2 January 1904.
218 Michael Madden personal communication.
219 *Cork Examiner.* 2 January 1904.
220 B.T. & R. Larn. *Shipwreck Index of Ireland.*
221 *Historic Shipwrecks of the East & West Cork Coast, Dúchas:* The Heritage Service, 2000.

being southerly in thick visibility and the tide ebbing. They sailed further in the bay in a northerly direction and the main sheet carried away, thus preventing them from bearing off and they had to let in further to find smoother water, in the belief that they were inside Cork Harbour. In vain they tried to anchor to bring the vessel head to wind, but they grounded on the White Strand in the early hours of Christmas morning. They launched their tender and went ashore at 2pm. The vessel was lying on an even keel in a good position and no immediate damage to it was evident. The cause of the casualty was put down to mistaking the new light at the Old Head for Roche's Point. This statement was received by W.D. Richards, Receiver of Wrecks.[222]

The *Rob Roy* was later re-floated and saved. On St Stephen's Day, a Queenstown tug failed to pull the vessel off. However, it was reported in the Cork Examiner on 2 January, 1908, that she was re-floated and towed to Youghal.

Bedouin: A 79-ton schooner from Baltimore was lost after colliding with an unknown steam trawler, 12 miles southwest of the Old Head on 17 June 1908. This vessel was out of Skibbereen for Newport, carrying a crew of four under Captain W. Nolan, wind conditions northeast force 2.[223]

Macks: This 5-ton lugger broke from her moorings at the Old Head on 8 December 1910. Her crew was ashore and the ship became a total loss.[224]
Position 51.38.49 N 08.32.67 W

Falls of Garry: 22 April 1911.

The *Falls of Garry* went aground on the Quay Rock in the early hours of the morning of 22 April 1911. The vessel, a 2026-ton steel four-masted barque, took the bottom in an exposed area of coastline west of Cuas *Mór* at the western entrance of Oysterhaven. The vessel carried a crew of 25 including three apprentices and a large cargo of wheat. She had left Port Pirie in South Australia on October 26 and was bound for Queenstown, now Cobh. Head winds and poor visibility hampered her passage for the previous fourteen days. On the last evening of the voyage a dense fog accompanied by strong southwesterly winds made for precarious conditions.

> 'Last night the Old Head of Kinsale light was observed and the fog signal on the coast could be heard distinctly. At 8pm. She was under foresails, and, as the men state, hove to for a pilot. Later on in the night, or a few minutes before one o'clock this morning, the scurrying of footsteps on deck and shouting of the watch on duty woke some of the watch below, and a few minutes after all hands were called on deck. The dreaded cry was for the moment misunderstood, as the reasons had not been made clear to the watch below, but as they reached the deck in their night attire they soon realised that their ship was nearing the land...The breakers on the iron rock-bound coast of the Sovereigns soon conveyed to all hands that the ship was doomed......All hands set to work and backed the yards, but owing to the blinding fog, with rain and sea breaking over the ship, no trace of land could be seen, and though all realised that the rocks were within the immediate vicinity, their

222   Depositions. *Register of Examinations on Oath concerning Wrecks and Casualties on the Coasts of the United Kingdom* by the Receiver of Wrecks for the district of Kinsale, 448th section of the Merchant Shipping Act 1884. Marine Department Committee.
223   B.T. & R. Larn. *Shipwreck Index of the Irish Coast.*
224   Ibid.

whereabouts could not be discerned. Then arrangements were made to let go the anchors, but it was useless. Sail was shortened and foresails were taken in, and still there was doubt, but it was soon after set to rest as the fine ship bumped heavily forward and threw men off their feet as she did so. There was now no longer doubt, for the *Falls of Garry* was ashore and firmly held forward'.[225]

The captain, who was named Roberts, for some unknown reason did not take a pilot on board when he lay hove - to the east of the Old Head. There were two pilot cutters in the vicinity, the *Maid of Erin* and the *Morning Star*. The starboard watch who had had a gruelling day, had only gone down below to rest, a couple of hours before land was sighted, looming out of the poor visibility. When the ship grounded, the captain called for the starboard lifeboat to be launched. Thirteen of the crew boarded the lifeboat and while lowering in dangerous conditions many of the personal effects and lifeboat cargo were washed overboard. The crew had to hack the hoist ropes with a hatchet to clear the attachment to the ship to make a safe getaway. Having got clear, they remained on stand-by as the port lifeboat was launched. The port lifeboat proved more problematic as it broke adrift with only six men on board when the vessel was being launched. This left the captain and five remaining crewmen on board. The captain insisted on staying on board but insisted that the five crewmen left should be taken off; however, this proved impossible given the sea conditions at the time. The port lifeboat proved very difficult for six men to work the oars (they only managed a quarter of a mile in six hours). They met up with one of the pilot cutters who advised against trying to get alongside the stricken vessel. The pilot cutter brought them to Oysterhaven and went back to rescue the six others from the ship using the rocket apparatus. The starboard lifeboat eventually with its 13 occupants reached Cobh after a tiresome struggle and they were later reunited with their shipmates who were brought there from Oysterhaven. Thirteen years prior to this the vessel had been involved in a similar incident:

> On 22 February 1898 the *Falls of Garry* had been driven into a coral reef at Ichino, New Caledonia and was sold for £47 being considered a total loss. The ship was salvaged by Mr Thompson of Sydney who blasted away the coral reef and re-floated her a year later with a false bottom. The *Falls of Garry* had been sold again to Copen, Craig and Walker of Glasgow and was en route to her new owners. Captain Roberts was suspended for six months as a result of the loss.[226]

Today artefacts from the vessel can be seen at Kinsale museum.

⬦ Fig.39: *Falls of Garry* which was lost near Ballymacus Point in 1911. *Courtesy of Christy Fitzgerald*

225 *Cork Examiner*, 24 April 1911.
226 Bourke, E. *Shipwrecks of the Irish Coast* 11 May 1993. Power Press, Dublin 1994.

Anglo-Colombian: A British cargo ship of 4,792 tons was sunk by gunfire from a German submarine in position 51 00.07'N 08 42.97'W, on 23 September 1915. She was out from Quebec to Avonmouth with a cargo of horses.[227]

Hesione: Another British cargo ship sunk on the same day as the aforementioned by the U-41, a German submarine. This vessel of 3,364 tons was on a voyage from the Clyde to Buenos Aires with general cargo. There were no casualties.[228]

Earl of Lathom: a wooden square-rigged three-masted schooner of 132 registered tons. Her port of registry was Liverpool, England. She had a crew of five. In the first week of May 1915, she was carrying a cargo of bacon and potatoes from Limerick to Liverpool. The *U-20* stopped the vessel sometime after 2a.m. on Wednesday, 5 May 1915. The submarine commander ordered the crew of the schooner to abandon ship and bring him the ship's flag and papers. The crew of the captured cargo ship complied. As the crew headed for the shore in their lifeboat, the *U-20* launched 12 grenades at the schooner before the vessel heeled over and sank.[229]

⚓ Fig40: *Earl of Lathom*, lost off the Old Head in 1915. *Author's Collection.*

The lifeboat and crew were later picked up by the Arklow steam drifter *Daniel O'Connell*, which witnessed the sinking and landed the survivors at Kinsale. This vessel rescued 60 passengers two days later when the *Lusitania* was torpedoed nearby.[230] The approximate position for the wreck is 51 28' 50'N 08 34'39'W

227   www.wrecksite.eu
228   Ibid.
229   D. Hickey & G. Smith. *Seven Days to Disaster.* G.P. Putnam's Sons, 1982.

Lusitania: 7 May 1915

So much has been written about this vessel already that only a selection of specifically chosen occurrences are included in this chapter. The following is the testimony of passenger J.H. Brooks of Connecticut who survived the ordeal.

"I was a saloon passenger and had only just come up from lunch. I went to the wireless deck, and was standing near the Marconi room when, happening to glance over the starboard side, I saw about 150 yards away the track of a torpedo which was rapidly approaching. I leaned over the rail, and saw it strike the ship under the bridge. Immediately a great volume of water was flung into the air, and I was violently thrown on the deck. Then there was a cloud of steam, which enveloped the entire fore part of the ship, which made it impossible to see. The impact lifted the bow of the ship on the port side, and then the vessel immediately settled back on a level keel, and began to settle down slowly to port. The vessel immediately took a sharp course towards Kinsale Head, and was travelling apparently at 17 knots. The ship took such a list to starboard that the port side boats were useless. There was no excitement or hysteria. The captain on the bridge, raised his hand and shouted there was no danger; 'Don't lower the boats.' Nevertheless, the crew, who were at the davits, continued their efforts to free them. Soon the boats from the top deck were floating on the water, which was not three feet below the deck. I assisted a number of ladies into the boats, and after that went to get into the last boat, but when I saw how the ship was going down, I dived off the starboard side, and swam quickly away from her. As I did so, the Marconi wire fell across me, and nearly dragged me under. As she went under, the wash brought a collapsible boat towards me, and I and three others got into it. We pulled in a number of women and men who were floating near it. The boat had no oars, and the collapsible sides could not be raised to the full height, but we propped them up as full as we could, and fished six floating oars in from the sea. Long before this, the *Lusitania* had disappeared. She went down bow first, and the funnel struck several boats and numbers of men, women and children who were struggling in the water, with many dead bodies in their midst. We rowed towards Kinsale Head, and were picked up by a Kinsale trawler.[231]

⚓ Fig.41: The *Lusitania. Author's Collection.*

230 *Cork Examiner.* 15 May 1915.
231 *Irish Times,* 7 May 1915.

To give one a perspective on the sheer size of the vessel, her dimensions were as follows : Length, 790ft.; Beam, 88ft.; Draft, 37ft.; Freeboard, 80ft.; Tonnage 45,000; Turbine engines 68,000 HP.

> The coal that feeds her boilers on one voyage between Liverpool and New York would fill 22 trains, each made up of thirty 10 ton trucks. The feeding of the crew and passengers reads something like the commissariat for a small town. Here are a few amongst the items- four hundred pigeons, two hundred and fifty partridges, two hundred and fifty grouse, eight hundred quail, two hundred snipe, sixty lambs, ten calves, forty oxen, two hundred pheasants, eighty sheep, two thousand fowl, one hundred and thirty pigs,, one hundred and fifty turkeys, three hundred and fifty ducks, ninety geese, and then of fish-twelve boxes of herrings, forty five boxes of turbot, sole, etc; sixty boxes of kippers, three hundred and twenty five lbs of turtles, two boxes of mackerel, twelve barrels of red herrings, fifteen hundred lbs of red salmon, thirty six boxes of bloaters, ten boxes of fresh herrings, eighty four boxes of haddock, twenty kegs of oysters, and 1.5 tons of ling.[232]

Eye-witness accounts from the headlands of the Old Head and Seven Heads were widespread, and the explosive sound had been heard by witnesses at Castlefreke, some distance to the west.

A farmer at work on the Old Head reported that he heard two shots about 2.15 p.m. and saw the vessels bow go up in the air . The great vessel sank between 15 and 20 minutes later.

NOTICE!

TRAVELLERS intending to embark on the Atlantic voyage are reminded that a state of war exists between Germany and her allies and Great Britain and her allies; that the zone of war includes the waters adjacent to the British Isles; that, in accordance with formal notice given by the Imperial German Government, vessels flying the flag of Great Britain, or of any of her allies, are liable to destruction in those waters and that travellers sailing in the war zone on ships of Great Britain or her allies do so at their own risk.

IMPERIAL GERMAN EMBASSY
WASHINGTON, D. C., APRIL 22, 1915.

⚓ Fig.42: Warning that appeared in the US press prior to the sailing of the *Lusitania*.

---

232   *Cork County Eagle & Munster Advertiser,* 8 May 1915.

⚓ Fig.43: The Manx fishing vessel 'Wanderer' as seen at the pier head in Kinsale .This
was the first vessel to arrive on the scene of the *Lusitania* after she was torpedoed –
she took passengers on board along with two lifeboats in tow saving 160 passengers.
Courtesy of Tony Bocking

About 4 o'clock the steam trawler *Daniel O'Connell*, that had been fishing about eight miles south-west of the Old Head, came on the scene and picked up two of the ship's boats which were about the spot. Those contained 65 passengers, mostly women and children, all of whom were in a deplorable condition. The trawler was taking those survivors to Kinsale, but was intercepted by a government tug, which took them to Queenstown. Great excitement prevails in Kinsale, but not a single passenger has arrived there. The steam trawler *Daniel O'Connell*, it will be remembered, rescued the crew of the three- masted schooner, the *Earl of Latham* on Wednesday last, after that boat had been torpedoed eight miles south-southwest of Kinsale.[233]

Another Kinsale-based Manx fishing vessel was the first in place at the location. The *Wanderer,* under William Ball, was at the scene for two hours before any other vessel appeared. He took on board 160 passengers, some of whom stayed in the two ship's lifeboats that the fishing smack took in tow. These were transferred to another vessel, the *Flying Fish,* which landed the victims in Queenstown.[234]

Today the wreck lies in a northeast, southwest direction, just over eleven miles southwest of the Old Head. Thirty years ago the depth recorded on the echo sounder from the top of the wreck lying on its side to the bottom was 10 fathoms. Today the height of the wreck is much less than this as it has collapsed over time. In the interim it has attracted the attention of divers, explorers, anglers looking for specimen wreck fish, such as white and black pollock, ling and cod. It has also provided commercial fishermen with large catches of some of the above species which find sanctuary on the wreck site. The big questions that are still unanswered are whether the vessel was carrying munitions, and what caused the second explosion immediately after the first? The legend of the *Lusitania* lives on.

At the inquest in Kinsale that followed, the jury were told that the naval ship *Stormcock* intercepted the Arklow vessels *Daniel O'Connell* and *Elizabeth*, and demanded they hand over their passengers. Given that the boats were a short distance from Kinsale, and over 1.5 hours from Queenstown, this would not seem to make any sense. However, it is widely believed that the reasoning behind this was the British naval authority wanted complete control over the whole affair. It seems remarkable today that the town of Kinsale, given its proximity to the sinking, played a secondary role to Queenstown in the whole incident.

The naval authorities in Queenstown did not favour the inquest being held in Kinsale. In Queenstown they could drive their own agenda, but this was not the case in Kinsale because of nationalist elements in that town. Coroner Horgan, a nationalist, presided over the inquest in Kinsale, and the naval authorities were afraid that he would expose the cover ups made by the naval command. They recalled the *Juno*, the naval flagship of the Irish coast patrol, soon after she left Cork Harbour. This was a very reckless decision given that the authorities knew about submarine activity in the area and the vulnerability of the *Lusitania*. The *Juno* was sent to protect the *Lusitania* and they had

233   *Cork Examiner,* 8 May 1915.
234   *Cork Examiner,* 13 May 1915.

given instructions for the ship to come into Queenstown. They wanted a scapegoat, and Captain Turner was who they had in mind. As it happened, Coroner Horgan squarely laid the blame on the German U-Boat and not on Turner, who the Admiralty wanted to make a sacrificial lamb.[235]

For weeks afterwards bodies were found, from the Old Head to as far away as the Aran Islands. There were some poignant reminders in the press in the days that followed, photographs of missing passengers being sought by their grieving families and rewards offered to fishermen if they managed to retrieve their loved ones.

Thomasina: Shelled and sunk 40 miles south-southeast of the Old Head on 10 June 1915. A Russian sailing ship under ballast, she had a warning shell fired across her bows by a German submarine and the crew were ordered to take to her boats. Seven shells were fired at the vessel and she sank within thirty minutes. The crew, including the captain, consisting of 17 Russians, two Swedes and one Norwegian, rowed for seven hours and were picked up by the steamship *Polandia*.[236]
The vessels recorded position is 51 02.32'N 07 45.23'W.[237]

Oakwood: Sunk by gunfire 45 miles south-southeast of the Old Head on 11 August 1915. This 4,279-ton steamship was en route from Liverpool to Cienfuegos (Cuba) under ballast with a crew of thirty-five, when the crew was ordered to abandon ship by the commander of a German submarine U-8. The master of the vessel ordered full steam ahead. However, the engine was soon put out of commission and the crew abandoned ship. The U-Boat shelled the vessel further until it sank. The crew of the ship were picked up by a naval vessel shortly afterwards and were landed in Queenstown.[238]
The vessels recorded position is 50 56.06'N   08 06. 37' W.[239]

---

235 Tony Bocking personal communication.
236 www. Irishshipwrecks.com
237 www.wrecksite.eu
238 B. T & R. Larn, *Shipwreck Index of the Irish Coast.*
239 www. wrecksite.eu

⚓ Fig.44: *Arabic*- sunk off the Seven Heads in 1915. *Author's Collection.*

Arabic: Torpedoed and sank by the U-20 or U-14 with a loss of 44 lives, 48 miles south-southwest of the Old Head, on 19 May 1915, with a loss of 44 lives. This vessel of 15,501 tons was reputed to be carrying a quantity of gold and diamonds. Position 50 56.53'N 08 9.21'W.[240]

> The *Arabic* was proceeding on a zig-zag course making 16 knots when the *SS. Dunsley* was sighted up ahead on fire shortly after 9.00 am. As the ships closed, it was seen that the *Dunsley* was down by the head, and that there were two boats pulling away from her. When between 2-3 miles off, the second officer saw the wake of a torpedo heading for them when only some 200 yards away, but despite putting the helm hard to starboard the torpedo hit him 100ft from the stern. The engine was stopped and the ship took a list to starboard, then came upright and then began to settle down. She sank at 9.42 am, ten minutes after being torpedoed. There was no time to launch the main lifeboats, but the collapsible boats and rafts floated clear on their own and saved many lives. Patrol boats picked up the survivors and landed them in Queenstown.[241]

New York City: 2,970 gross tons, sunk by gunfire 35 miles south of the Old Head on 19 August 1915.

> This steamship was captured by the German submarine U-24, her crew forced to abandon her without loss of life, after which the vessel was sunk by gunfire. She was chased for an hour and a half by the enemy vessel, during which time the enemy fired continually, one shell hitting the bridge at 3pm. The master decided to abandon ship and the crew took to the boats at 4.30 pm. Once the survivors were clear, the submarine again opened fire and continued to shell the steamship until she sank. The survivors were picked up by the *SS. Lily* and landed at Queenstown the next morning.[242]

Dunsley: A steamship of 4,930 tons carrying general cargo, was sunk close to the *Arabic* on the same day, about 48 miles southwest of the Old Head. Position 50 55.06'N 08 17.88'W.

> This steamship was captured by the German submarine U-24, her crew forced to abandon ship, after which she was sunk by gunfire.[243]

---

240 Ibid.
241 B.T & R. Larn. *Shipwreck Index of the Irish Coast.*
242 Ibid.
243 Ibid.

Bradford: A 163-ton trawler on war patrol was lost in a gale off the Old Head on 28 October 1916.

> This Grimsby trawler was hired by the Admiralty in 1915, converted to a patrol vessel and armed, No 829, and was lost during a gale off the Old Head of Kinsale with all hands, consisting of one officer and eleven naval ratings.[244]

Nailsea Court: This 3,295-ton ship was shelled by a German submarine 32 miles south by east of the Old Head on 19 January 1917.[245]

Storenes: This 1,870-ton Norwegian barque was captured by a German submarine off the Old Head on 1 March 1917, and sunk by explosive scuttling charges after the crew were forced to abandon ship. The skippers name was Hansen.[246]

Marbella: Another Norwegian ship of 1,637 tons was sunk in similar circumstances to the aforementioned on the same day, 22 miles south-southwest of the Old Head.[247]

Larfostenes: Abandoned and scuttled, 35 miles southeast by south of the Old Head on 9 March 1917. A 2,118- ton Norwegian steamship, out of New York for Rotterdam. The vessel was stopped by a German submarine, the U-53, her crew forced to abandon ship and she was sunk by explosive scuttling charges.[248]

Circe: A French vessel of 4,133 tons was torpedoed by the U-70 on 15 March 1917, after the crew had abandoned the vessel 65 miles south-southeast of the Old Head. The crew were forced to take to the boats and the vessel was initially shelled. When this failed to sink her, she was torpedoed.[249]

Gafsa: A tanker of 3,974 tons was torpedoed 8-10 miles southeast of the Old Head on 28 March 1917.

> Ex-(*Dominion*). This Admiralty oiler was torpedoed and sunk with the loss of seven lives by the German submarine U-57. She was torpedoed at 5.15p.m. Whilst being escorted by a Royal Navy warship, the weapon exploding in the engine room killing seven of the engine room staff. The remainder of the crew abandoned ship and got away immediately in two boats, being picked up by the escorting vessel. At no time was the enemy submarine seen, and since she sank so quickly whilst carrying 4,900 tons of fuel oil cargo, it is possible she was struck simultaneously by two torpedoes at the same time. The survivors were landed at Queenstown.[250]

Position 51.29.42 N 08.19.42 W

244 Ibid.
245 *Historic Shipwrecks of the East & West Cork Coast.*
246 B.T & R. Larn, *Shipwreck Index of Ireland.*
247 Ibid.
248 Ibid.
249 Ibid.
250 Ibid.

Imataka: A 1,776-ton steamship carrying a cargo of frozen meat, rum and sugar was torpedoed 10 miles southeast of the Old Head on 23 April 1917.

> Whilst proceeding alone at 8.5 knots, this submarine was torpedoed in hold No 2 at 0.45 am, by the German submarine UC-47. The crew and passengers abandoned ship in three boats at 1. 15 am., the master remained with the ship until she sank at 3.30am. The submarine came to the surface and passed very close to the Chief Officer's boat, then made off on the surface at full speed. The boat holding the master and other members of the crew were picked up by warships and landed at Queenstown.[251]

The remnants of this ship are found in the approximate position 51.29.58'N 08.27.00'W.[252]

Madura: A Norwegian barque of 1096 tons was carrying a cargo of timber to Cardiff from Gulfport on 21 May 1917 when she was scuttled by a German submarine, U-48. Two crew members were lost.[253]

Lillian H: Scuttled by explosives, 15 miles south of the Old Head, on 19 June 1917. This 473-ton schooner was en route from Whitehaven to Barbados with a cargo of roofing slates when the crew were forced to abandon ship by a German submarine and subsequently scuttled.[254]
The vessel lies in the approximate position 51.21.67 N and 08.27.35 W, about 5 miles southeast of the *Lusitania*.

Spectator: A 3,808-ton steamship torpedoed 6.25 miles southwest of the Seven Heads on 19 August 1917. Out of Cape Town for Liverpool with a general cargo including copper and sheet bar. She carried 45 crew under Captain J. McMullan.

> Torpedoed and sunk by the German submarine UC-33 without loss of life, the vessel was proceeding on a zig-zag course at 9.5 knots, escorted by the USN torpedo boat destroyer, *Paulding*. The torpedo which sank the steamer was seen approaching on the port side from abeam when only 20 yards away. It detonated between No's 2 & 3 holds, destroying both forward lifeboats and her wireless aerials. She was attacked at 10. 18 am. began to settle immediately, and unable to stop her engine since the space had become flooded, orders were given to abandon ship, 43 of the crew getting away in the boats, the 2nd officer having to jump into the sea before he was picked up. The master went down with the ship, but managed to surface and was also rescued, the ship being under water within 8 minutes of being hit. The same submarine sunk the SS. *Akassa* only six days previous. Part of her cargo consisting of bar copper, which attracted the attention of the Italian salvage ship *Artiglio* between 1934-35, which was the same vessel that successfully recovered gold from the wreck of *the SS. Egypt*, in the Bay of Biscay. The escort picked up the survivors, landing them in Queenstown.[255]

The *Spectator* is now well broken up after various salvage expeditions over the years and lies in position 51.28.17 N 08.41.87 W.

---

251   Ibid.
252   www.wrecksite.eu
253   Ibid.
254   B.T & R. Larn, *Shipwreck Index of Ireland*.
255   Ibid.

Elsa: A 1,236-ton Danish barque, was sunk by a German submarine after the crew abandoned the ship six miles south of the Old Head on 9 September 1917. This vessel was carrying a 1,601 ton cargo of coal and the master's name was Thorson.[256] The approximate position of this wreck is 51.30.25 N 08'31'96 W.[257]

East Wales: A 4,321-ton steamship in ballast, was shelled and sunk by a German submarine on 14 October 1917, after her crew were forced to abandon ship. Three of her crew were killed in the shelling.[258]
The vessel lies in 47 fathoms and is still discernable on the echo sounder about 10 miles east-southeast of the Old Head and 3 miles southeast of the Ling Rocks. The latitude and longitude of this wreck is 51.33.00 N 08.15.70 W.

Lynton: A Finnish barque of 2,531 tons was torpedoed and sunk by a German submarine U-48 at 50 37.20'N 08 23.17'W on 21 May 1917.[259]

SS Gamma: Lost at 51 07.94'N 08 38.09'W in 1917.[260]

SS Marmora: Lost at 50 41.71'N 08 33.02'W in 1918.[261]

Etonian: A ship of 6,515 tons was torpedoed and sank 34 miles south by east of the Old Head on 23 March 1918. Seven crew were lost.[262]

Waneta: A 1,683-ton tanker was sunk by a German submarine 42 miles south-southeast of the Old Head, whilst carrying a cargo of fuel oil, on 30 May 1918.[263]

Konarky: December 1918. Surviving accounts for the final hours of the *Konarky* come from third officer William Mitchell of Sun View Villas, Douglas Road, Cork.
About 9pm on Sunday, some sixteen miles off Galley Head, a collision took place between two vessels, both vessels showing full lights at the time. The vessel *Ordura* hit the *Konarky* nearly at right angles on the port side, killing seven men and wrecking the engine room as well as all lighting arrangements. This also affected the radio communication system and put it beyond use. The survivors were transferred to the *Ordura*, while the captain and officers remained aboard the *Konarky* until they were ordered to leave by the captain of the British sloop. The *Konarky* then drifted into shore at Courtmacsherry Bay in the vicinity of Garretstown Strand.[264]
The section that is visible at low water on a spring tide is that of the bow of the vessel. It is thought that another part of the wreck lay further out in the bay, but this has not been confirmed. The vessel lies in position 51 38.23'N 08 35.04'W, and is evident at low water on a spring tide, with a section of the vessel visible just above the water.

256   Ibid.
257   www.wrecksite.eu
258   B.T. & R. Larn, *Shipwreck Index of Ireland.*
259   www.wrecksite.eu
260   Ibid.
261   Ibid.
262   *Historic Shipwrecks of the East & West Cork Coast.*
263   B.T & R. Larn, *Shipwreck Index of Ireland.*
264   *Cork Examiner,* 5 December 1918.

⚓ Fig.45: *Cardiff Hall* which was lost at the Seven Heads in 1925. *Author's Collection.*

Cardiff Hall: 13 January 1925.

The *Cardiff Hall* looms large in the consciousness of the populace of the Seven Heads. The main factors that contribute to this are the totality of life lost at this tragic occurrence and the notoriety of the Shoonta rock, which it struck on the southeast corner of the Seven Heads. Nowadays one is constantly reminded of that event when passing through the village of Butlerstown where the anchor from the stricken vessel is on display. From the clifftop above the fatal spot, a two ton section of the hull remains to be seen to this day.

The event is known in the locality as 'the night of the *Cardiff Hall'*.
The dimensions of the vessels were 350 x 50.8 x 25.6 ft.[265]
The vessel had a triple expansion engine of about 300hp and a speed of 9 knots.[266]

265 www.irishshipwrecksonline.net
266 John N. Jordan. *Sea Breezes*, 15 January 2010. Sea Breezes Publications Ltd.

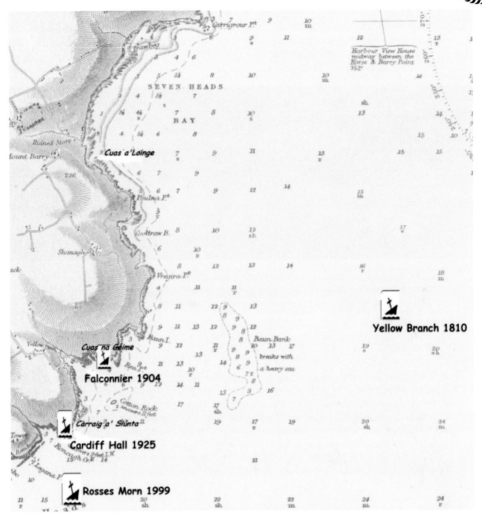

Yellow Branch 1810

Falconnier 1904

Cardiff Hall 1925

Rosses Morn 1999

⚓ Fig.46: Chart of the south-eastern corner of the Seven Heads indicating known and approximate wreck sites.

The following is what appeared in the press on the days that followed the disaster:

Information has been received in Cork that the ship that went ashore off Clonakilty on Tuesday evening during the unprecedented storm was the *Cardiff Hall*, owned by Messrs. W.A. Young and Co., Ltd, London.

Mr Rohan, of Messrs. Scotts, Shipping Agents, telegraphed the Harbour Master yesterday for particulars of the ship which was reported to have gone ashore, and received a reply that the only thing that was known about it was the name *Cardiff Hall*, and that one body had been washed ashore. The coast at this point is so treacherous that during a fierce storm such as prevailed on Tuesday, any vessel that was manageable, and with the sea that was running, had practically no chance, and it would be miraculous if there were even any survivors. The *Cardiff Hall* had a registered tonnage of 2,540, and was on a voyage from Rosario, River Plate (Argentina), with a cargo of 6,000 tons of maize, consigned to Messrs. R& H. Hall, Ltd., Cork, valued for about £70,000.

Fig.47: The south-eastern corner of the Seven Heads, showing Ballymacredmond signal tower on the far left. The *Cardiff Hall* struck *Carraig a'Siúnta*, marked by red star in the foreground. The *Falconnier* was lost at *Cuas na Géime,* marked by a red star on the right hand side of image. *Courtesy of Kevin Dwyer.*

A visit yesterday to the scene brought to light some additional particulars of the tragic loss on Tuesday night off the West Cork coast of the SS. *Cardiff Hall.* There is unfortunately no doubt that every soul on board was lost, for within half an hour from striking, a few scattered pieces of broken timber were all that remained of the ship. The scene of the disaster was a little cove called Travara Bay. It is about seven miles west of the Old Head of Kinsale and is a portion of that strip of rocky coastline known as the Seven Heads. The bay runs in perhaps a couple of hundred yards and from point to point across its mouth measures about five hundred yards. In the centre of which distance is the Cotton Rock. It was just off the western point that the *Cardiff Hall* came ashore.

Here about fifty yards off the mainland is the Shoonta Rock, which is uncovered to the extent of several feet at low tide. The precipitous cliff which constitutes the nearest mainland is the point at the western side of the bay. The whole coast is extremely rocky and huge cliffs rise almost sheer from the water's edge in most places. The mainland just opposite the Shoonta Rock is indented by a tremendous cleft several feet across and running some fifteen or twenty yards landwards. Some little distance west is an old tower in which it was customary up to about three years ago to have a watch light burning. No light burns there now.

As far as it is possible to reconstruct the manner in which the disaster occurred, the *Cardiff Hall* drifting from the east and not under control was driven shorewards by the furious southerly gale and her bows just cleared the Shoonta Rock. Her stern however struck, and this caused her bow to swing shoreward until it became jammed on the outer edge of the cleft in the cliff already referred to. The next wave landed the stern on to the Shoonta Rock and within a few minutes-even seconds-the vessel was broken into two. A quarter of an hour later nothing more was to be seen.

When our representative visited the scene yesterday-a clear calm day- the seas outside had greatly moderated, but even then waves lashed against the rocky coast with appalling fury, flinging immense clouds of spray a hundred feet high. The conditions the previous night can be better imagined than described, but some inkling of the mighty force of the seas may be gleaned from two facts. The cliff at the edge of the mainland is anything from 120 to 150 ft. high and not alone were clouds of spray hurled over it during the storm, but a short time after the wreck large quantities of maize were thrown up this huge distance and carried a hundred yards or more inland. The top of the cliff was yesterday strewn with the meal. Another illustration may be given. A huge mass of twisted iron, weighing about two tons, assumed to be a portion of the vessel's keel, was hurled forty feet above the water's edge on to the rocks, where it still remains. Even yesterday with only moderate seas running a mile off shore, mighty waves thundered against the Shoonta Rock and threw huge columns of water on to the shore on the mainland. Six young men, resident in the locality, being anxious no doubt to make a closer examination of that portion of the vessel's keel already referred to, clambered down the rocks and were unable to retreat in time from a gigantic wave which buried them for a moment. Had they not held on with the utmost tenacity to the rocks, they must have shared the fate of the unfortunate crew of the lost steamer.

Interviewed by an 'Examiner' representative yesterday some of those who were at the cliff's edge during the wreck gave graphic descriptions of the loss of the vessel and the efforts-hopeless from the start-at rescues. Mr Patrick Aherne, who lives only a hundred yards away, told our reporter that he first saw the ship coming from an easterly direction and travelling slowly, as if being carried along by the tide. This was about eight o'clock on Tuesday night, when the steamer was about two miles off the coast. The wind, however, was driving her ashore. It was a very bad night with a ferocious gale raging and heavy rain obscuring the vision. All they saw of the ship were her two masthead lights and some idea of her size may be gleaned from the fact that Mr Aherne first thought there were two vessels, one standing by the other. In his opinion she was disabled and out of control. Her engines did not appear to be working. Mr Aherne thought the captain of the vessel must have been able to see the Old Head light six miles astern of him, but whether the land nearby was visible to those on the steamer was a matter of extreme doubt owing to the thick night and the driving rain and spray. It was an hour after Mr Aherne saw the steamer's lights that the vessel struck, as far as could be seen, in the manner already described. The siren was being sounded continuously, and after the steamer struck a boatswain's whistle was heard several times. Mr Aherne and those with him brought lanterns as near as they could to the cliff's edge, but could see practically nothing.

Piteous cries for help came up to them from the darkness at the foot of the cliff, but so bad were the conditions that it was not possible to stay at the cliff's edge. When it was evident that the ship was going ashore, messages were sent for the rocket apparatus three miles away, at Barry's Cove, and to the lifeboat station at Barry's Point about two and a half miles away, and several braved the terrible storm to try and procure assistance. The frantic appeals for help which the watchers on the cliff could not answer, continued only a few minutes and then all was silent save for the fury of the gale and the pounding of the seas over the vessel's grave.

"In less than an hour" said Mr Aherne, "there was not a trace of her left". From the start there was not the remotest chance of rescue, for even if the rocket apparatus was there when she struck, there would have been time to take off only three or four hands. When

267   *Cork Examiner.*15 January 1925.
268   *Cork Examiner.*16 January 1925.

the vessel was ashore we could get a glimpse of her now and then, but immediately huge waves washed over her, and in a few minutes nothing remained. It was when the crew saw the lights on the cliff that the whistle sounded and the cries for help were heard. Mr. James Hurley, the chief officer of the Barry's Cove Station, Coast Lifesaving Service, told our representative that he received news by telephone from Lislevane at 9.45p.m., that a vessel had gone ashore at Travara Bay. He immediately ordered out his rocket crew of 14 men, and they reached Travara Bay about 11.30 p.m. Mr. Aherne and a Mr. John McCarthy brought him to the scene of the wreck, not a trace of which was left. He searched for more than an hour, but nothing was to be seen owing to blinding spray and rain. "The place" he added, "is one of the wildest places I ever saw". He made a close search for a lifebuoy or any clue as to the identity of the vessel, but failed in his quest. The lifeboat at Barry's Point was also launched, although it was obvious that she would be able to get around the point, and to attempt to reach the scene would be utterly futile. Nevertheless, a crew stood by in readiness, but unfortunately were unable to render assistance. Even if a lifeboat were available at Travara Bay and was then launched, nothing could be done owing to the position of the wrecked steamer offering no lee shore, and to the fact that she broke up in a few minutes.

Up to last evening two bodies had only come ashore. The first, that of a handsome looking and finely proportioned grey headed man, attired only in singlet and socks, and with a bandage on the head, was washed ashore in the bay, six hundred yards away an hour after the wreck and was found by John Kirby of Shannaugh. There was a very deep gash in the forehead, and the whole body was badly bruised. The second body, that of a small man, also undressed, was frightfully mutilated about the head, and one leg was fractured, with the bones protruding through the flesh. This body came ashore about 10 o'clock yesterday morning, and was discovered by John Fleming, one of the volunteer company in the Coast Lifesaving Service. The remains were found a mile east of the wreck at Shannaugh Point. Approaching the scene of the disaster yesterday one met with scores of horse and donkey drawn vehicles coming away from the beach with broken timbers and loads of maize. The scene at Travara Bay itself normally a wild and desolate spot- was one of almost feverish industry, and hundreds of carts of all descriptions kept coming and going all day. Down on the rocky beach, with the tide low, scores of men and boys with buckets, pans, saucepans, and every similar utensil were gathering up the grain that came ashore in bucketful's with every wave. Standing on the cliff overlooking the little bay, one saw the men running out after each wave, then dragging a bucket or pan across the beach and hurrying back before the next wave broke. On the rocks at both sides of the bay were other parties who lowered buckets and bags down to the workers below, where they were quickly filled, hauled to the top, emptied into a cart, and sent down empty again. Back a little from the shore was another large party having a picnic dinner before resuming work. The narrow rocky and muddy road which wound down to the innermost point of the rocky beach was crowded with vehicles moving up and down. High up on the rocks and at the sides of this road were heaps of maize awaiting removal and piles of battered timbers, each piece significantly less than six feet long. For miles around were carts to be seen, large and small, returning homeward with meal or timber or perhaps bound for the beach for more. One could scarcely believe that so isolated a district could have produced the number of men, animals and carts engaged in the salvage work. From dawn until dusk the work went on unceasingly, and even after nightfall many were still engaged in removing the heaps of meal stored in the hurry of the day anywhere above the high water mark. All day, too, came women and children with food for their menfolk and to assist as far as possible with the work. The bed of the bay had assumed a dull gold colour of maize mixed with sand-a mixture that was easily separated when bought ashore.

A very sad sight that sharply brought home to the minds of those who witnessed it, the terrible loss of life which attended the wreck, and the savage fury of the elements, was the presence in the long procession of carts coming from the beach of two donkey carts, each containing one of the mutilated and blood-stained bodies of the ill-fated crew of the wrecked steamer. The first was covered by an international code signal flag and the second only by a piece of sacking, while being removed to the lookout hut at The Seven Heads. A few pieces of a broken lifebuoy that came ashore with the first body and a second lifebuoy subsequently washed ashore almost intact were also taken away for production at the inquest. Sergeant White, Courtmacsherry, and Sergeant Conway, Timoleague, were in charge of the Civic Guard party who made the necessary arrangements and who remained on duty at the bay during yesterday.

It was not possible to definitely ascertain the number of crew, but it is believed to be anything between 25 and 40.[267]

One of the residents of the district said it would be very advisable to have some effort made to get a light arranged, for in that part of the coast ships often came ashore there, and it was a very dangerous place. The Coroner (Neville, solicitor, Bandon) said this was a matter which should be brought to the notice of the government.[268]

The two bodies upon which the inquest was held on Thursday afternoon were to have been interred yesterday, but burial was delayed on receipt of a message that relatives of the captain of the s.s. *Cardiff Hall* were on their way and would reach Butlerstown in the afternoon. The two gentlemen in question were Mr. Thomas Bowen, brother of Captain Bowen and Mr A.T.Arthur, brother in law, who had come from Wales under the impression from the press descriptions that the first body-that of the tall, grey-haired man-was that of the captain. This belief was confirmed on reaching Ireland, when Mr. Bowen purchased a copy of the *'Cork Examiner'* and in it saw the photograph of the dead man. Mr.Bowen told our representative that after seeing the photograph he no longer had the slightest doubt but that the body was that of his brother.

The remains will be taken to Cardiff for interment.They were removed to Clonakilty last night, and will be transferred, via Rosslare, to Wales today. The foundering of the s.s. *Cardiff Hall* is a double tragic event for Captain Bowen's widow and daughters, for the captain's only son, a fine young fellow of nineteen, was on board with him.

267   *Cork Examiner.*15 January 1925.
268   *Cork Examiner.*16 January 1925.

The officers and the crew of the ill-fated Cardiff Hall, numbering 28, and who were signed on at Newport last September, were as follows:-

Officers

Master-Captain D.J. Bowen, First Mate- T.H. Jones, Second Mate-B. Lloyd, Third Mate-J. Price. Chief Engineer- G. Elvidge. Second Engineer-J. Parker. Third Engineer-M.H. Anthony.

Crew

J. Gough, boatswain. T. Bowen, A.B.(the captain's son). I.J. Jones, A.B. A. Krusenberg, A.B. P.Lasten, A.B. K. Nurwell, A.B. F. Bonter, stewart. James Kavanagh, stewart. W. Sullivan, cabin boy. Taleb Salino, donkeyman. Mahen Ahmed, fireman. Hamed Massa, fireman. Ali Abraham, fireman. Abdul Mahomed, fireman. Said Abdulla, fireman. Mookbil Mahomed, fireman. E.J. James. I. Jones. B.D. Wilkes, wireless operator. Abdul Hamed, fireman, who was left in hospital in Buenos Aires.

The Civic Guards on duty at Travara were handed a photograph of Captain Bowen, his dead son, and his wife and two daughters, with a view towards assisting identification should the body of the captain's son be washed ashore... Another sad feature of the disaster was that, in response to a wireless message from her husband announcing the time at which he expected to arrive, Mrs Bowen was actually on the point of leaving for Cork, when the terrible news reached her, that she had lost her husband and only son. It was the boy's first voyage with his father, and at the conclusion of the journey he had intended sitting his mate's certificate.[269]

The Ruddock family of Courtmacsherry, a boatbuilding family, who were involved in other enterprises as well, converted their machinery into a grain-mill and the maize was processed for animal feed.[270]

This salvage brought a degree of prosperity to the area for a short time after the event. An interesting observation by a renowned diver and maritime author, Paddy O'Sullivan of Bandon, is that the vessel had only one of her two propellers intact when the vessel was dived on. The second propeller was missing, but the lock nut and split were still in place. This might well explain the reason why the vessel steamed in to the west towards Travara, rather than her intended passage to the east and Cork harbour. The lack of one propeller would certainly hinder the steerage of the ship considerably and account for her foundering on *Carraigasíunta*.

---

269   *Cork Examiner.*17 January 1925.
270   *Step back in Time in Courtmacsherry.* Courtmacsherry Harbour Lifeboat History Group. 2014.

⚓ Fig.48: Propeller from the *Cardiff Hall* on the strand at Lower Cove/*Cuas Innell,* Kinsale. *Courtesy of Paddy O'Sullivan*

⚓ Fig.49: The anchor of the *Cardiff Hall* on display at Butlerstown. *Author's Collection.*

A further link with this area was revealed to me recently by Billy Lynch, a grandson of a crewman from Kinsale named Florence Connell who sailed on this vessel previously and possibly would have been aboard had the vessel not been delayed in Wales for one month prior to the second last voyage. The young man signed up on another ship, little knowing what lay in store for his former shipmates.

The vessel had a troublesome history in the years that preceded the disaster, having at one time been adrift in the Bay of Biscay for a considerable period of time with mechanical problems. The captain is said to have suggested that the last trip was going to be his final one on that vessel since it was due some badly needed maintenance. Little did he know that it was also going to be his final trip for an altogether different reason.[271] The anchor that is on display as one enters Courtmacsherry on the seaward side is the vessel's stern anchor and the anchor proper is on display in Butlerstown.

⚓ Fig.50: Captain John Bowen of the *Cardiff Hall* laid out, being transported from Travara in 1925. *Courtesy of Cork Examiner*

---

271 Paddy O'Sullivan personal communication.

Chapter VI: 1927-2013

Loophead: This 220-ton ship out of Limerick was lost off the Old Head en route from Barry to Limerick with coal on 28 October 1927.[272]

The wreck of the *Pearl*, 1927

The story of the wreck of the three-masted schooner named the *Pearl* at Garretstown on 19 December 1927 is one largely forgotten in local lore in that area of the Cork coast. This oversight may be attributed to the fact that only four lives were lost and the vessel did not belong to that locality. Other better known shipwrecks such as the *Lusitania* in 1915 and the *City of Chicago* in 1892 (no lives lost) loom greater in the consciousness of the local populace. What is intriguing about this vessel is the fact that it was blown so far off course, leading one to question what it was that contributed to it ending up in the northwest corner of Garretstown Strand. This was an interesting period in time as it was during this era that sail gave way to power-driven vessels, and the safety of vessels in adverse conditions was much improved. One could surmise that it was the limitations of sail that led to the foundering of the *Pearl* of Gloucester.

The *Pearl* was registered at the port of Gloucester, her official registration number was 58186 and her owner was William T Symonds of Cardiff. She was built of wood at Whitehaven by Shepherd and Leech in 1867. Her gross tonnage was 122 tons, her length was 82.6ft, and she is described as a schooner.[273] Originally described as a

⚓ Fig.51: The star nearest to the top of the image is where the *Pearl* was lost. The star to the left is the position for the tanker *Konarky,* which was lost nine years previously in 1918. The bow of the tanker also represented a hazard for the *Pearl*, as it breaks the surface of the water at low tide. *Courtesy of Kevin Dwyer.*

272　*Historic Shipwrecks of the East & West Cork Coast, Dúchas:* The Heritage Service, 2000.
273　Research@shipwrecks.uk.com

barquentine and later converted to a schooner, this was in keeping with developments in ship technology and the economics of the time. The fact that most commercial vessels of this period had already converted to steam-driven power, made the use of sail questionable from an economic perspective. A barquentine, having three or more masts, would have required additional crew to handle the extra sails, while a three-masted schooner would have managed adequately with three hands on deck, making it a more viable proposition for smaller vessels such as the *Pearl*.

> The weather conditions of December 1927 were 'mainly cold and wintry, allied with strong easterly winds and gales during the second half of the month, except for an interval of mild weather from the 21st to the 24th. [274]

The conditions synonymous with this sort of weather are dry with little rain and dark overcast skies. The weather report for the period states that on 16 - 21 December (estimated timeframe for departure to date of occurrence of shipwreck) it became very cold, temperatures remaining below freezing for this period over large areas.

Many observers remarked on the unusual prevalence of easterly winds during the month; at Southport the *Observer* states that:

> During the month, winds from easterly points were more prevalent than in any month during 56 years observation. Strong winds and gales occurred in southwest districts between the 10th - 12th December and on the 18th. [275]

The same source tells us that the wind strength at Pendennis Castle in Cornwall on 16-17 December was between 25 and 38 miles per hour for a duration of 63 hours prior to this (the *Pearl* was possibly in this area at the time). The newspapers of the day collectively refer to the wind being easterly, however chart and weather data reports have more accurately pinpointed the wind as veering between east by south (101) and southeast by south (145). German weather charts for this period further confirm this. [276]

It is the Author's intention in this discussion to illustrate that the wind being southeasterly instead of the reputed easterly is a key factor in the foundering of the *Pearl*. I will endeavour to eliminate the ambiguity that news reports have created by their assertion that the wind was easterly at the time.

> This three-masted topsail schooner (originally a barquentine) was wrecked in a southeasterly gale, and all hands lost, after she struck a reef at Garretstown. 'And the vessel was constantly swamped by very large waves'. [277]

This vital piece of information is contrary to our understanding of the event and was not mentioned by newspapers at the time. In easterly conditions, large waves would not be present at Garretstown, as the area is sheltered by the Old Head. It has not been fully ascertained where the vessel was bound for at this time. The vessel left Cardiff about a week before the fatal incident. It is evident that she had been adrift in the fierce gale

274   http//library.metoffice.gov.uk/record=b1352142-S1
275   ibid
276   http://www.wetterzentrale.de/topkarten/fssipeur.html
277   Research@shipwrecks.uk.com

for several days. 'It has also been established that she was a coal schooner and that her final trading route was between ports on the west coast of Britain'[278]. It would seem that she left Cardiff in a lightweight condition, as there was little evidence of her coal cargo at the fatal scene. From the various pieces of information available to us it seems she spent much of her time between Lancashire ports and Cornwall. The lack of evidence regarding the final voyage of the *Pearl* is best explained by Mr. A.C.Horne, H.C., Cobh, a Lloyd's agent, in an interview with the *Cork Examiner*. He stated that:

> She was a coasting vessel of a type of which no regular list is issued by Lloyd's. Therefore it was often impossible to trace their whereabouts. She was certainly bound from a Mersey or British Channel port, he said, and there could be no doubt that the cargo was coal. She probably came from Garston near Liverpool, which was a centre of coastal coal trading.[279]

The same source gives the list of the following crew members: Captain Ernest Gordon of Runcorn Cheshire; Reginald Cooke, aged 21, also of Runcorn; Monashire Richards, aged 38, British of Asian extraction; and an unnamed Oriental deckhand. The question we now have to ask is this: What happened between the time of departure from Cardiff, as quoted by the news report, and the arrival at the fatal shore at Garretstown one week later?

On the days leading up to the disaster we have a good record by means of archival weather charts. These adverse weather conditions are substantiated by the newspapers of that period. It appears that Europe was in the grip of atrocious weather conditions, with extremes of temperature and severe winds. Reports from Cobh on the day following the wreck of the *Pearl* state:

> All the shipping companies at Cove to-day report very heavy weather at sea, which has occasioned delay in the arrival of the liners. Wireless messages received from the liners state that they are fighting their way steadily against a very unfavourable Easterly gale, accompanied by tempestuous seas in the Atlantic.[280]

If the information regarding the vessel leaving Cardiff approximately one week before is examined, it goes some way towards explaining how the vessel ended up in Garretstown. If, as stated, the vessel's trading area was the west coast of Britain, then it was only intent on going in one of two directions. One option was southwest to Land's End and east along the English Channel. This hypothesis would not make a lot of sense, given the type of conditions that one would encounter, trying to sail close to the wind on rounding Land's End. It would be unlikely to round that point, putting the vessel at further risk by trying to tack along a windward shore. The other likely route was west around St David's Head and up the St George's Channel, to a Lancashire port

---

278   *Cork Examiner*, 4 January 1928.
279   *Cork Examiner*, 23 December 1927.
280   *Cork Examiner,* 20 December 1927.

(see fig 52), which was the vessel's normal route. Ships leaving port in adverse weather conditions often anchor up outside the port area prior to departure in order to wait for changing weather conditions, rather than lying at the quayside where port charges could have been occurred and crew sobriety issues might also have been encountered. With little change evident and patience wearing thin, they may have left the inner reaches of the Bristol Channel a day or two after their reported departure from Cardiff or at anchor in the Cardiff Roads.

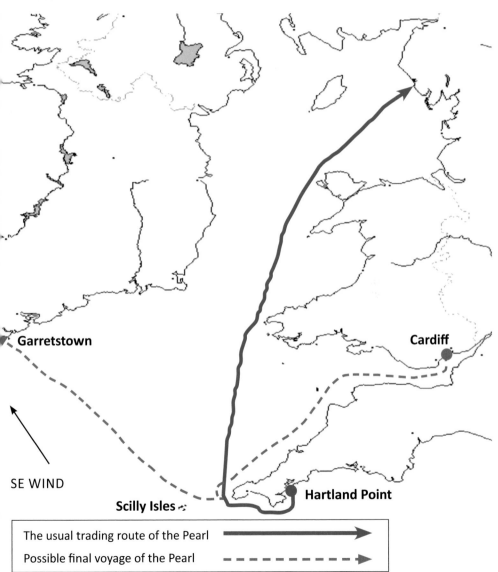

SE WIND

Garretstown

Cardiff

Scilly Isles

Hartland Point

| The usual trading route of the Pearl |
| Possible final voyage of the Pearl |

Fig.52: Map illustrating the last voyage of the *Pearl* 1927

An incidental comment on the state of the corpse of Captain Gordon says he had about five days beard growth when his body was retrieved.[281] This would suggest that he had his last shave at the quayside in Cardiff.

Leaving Cardiff (fig. 52) and tacking to the southwest in the relative shelter of the coastline from Weston-Super-Mare to Hartland Point in an easterly or south-easterly gale, with the wind abaft the port beam or on the port quarter, would have afforded relative comfort until the vessel got out of the shelter of the land, in this case the Bristol Channel. However, once west of the line of Carmarthen Bay to the north and Lands End to the south, the vessel was in a precarious position, due to the increased ferocity of the wind resulting from the lack of shelter previously offered when closer to land. This left the vessel to the mercy of the gale. The sudden increase in ferocity of the wind could easily have blown the sails out or torn them badly had sufficient reefs not been taken on the sails in on time. This would have seriously curtailed the manoeuvrability of the collier, and the only option open to the master would have been to run before the weather and avoid a beam sea (i.e. ship lying across the weather), which would have swamped the craft. This could have been done with the minimum of foresail. Using this hypothesis, a distance of two hundred and fifty miles of open water between Cardiff and the Old Head of Kinsale, at approximately 2 knots, in constrained circumstances could be achieved.

On reaching a point close to the Old Head of Kinsale in such conditions, it is very evident to any experienced mariner that Courtmacsherry Bay is a place to be approached with caution (fig. 53). On the west side of that bay, the shoal areas around the Baun bank, Carraigrour and *Carraig a'Shoonta* at the south-easterly point of the Seven Heads claimed all hands aboard the *Cardiff Hall* two years previously.[282] To the north of this is the Horse Rock and the mouth of the estuary of Courtmacsherry/ Timoleague, an area of shallows and sandbars and in extreme south-easterly conditions a place to be avoided. This estuary is the only opening in the bay that in suitable conditions would facilitate the safety of a vessel in such circumstances.

Courtmacsherry Harbour in the northwest corner of the bay, with its sandbar, narrow channels between sandbanks and strong tides, has never been a popular port for yachtsmen.[283] The middle and inside of Courtmacsherry Bay to the North and North East is strewn with reefs and shoals. The most notable of these reefs are the Outer and Inner Barrel Rocks in the middle of the bay. These are directly in a line if one was sailing from a point anywhere within a mile from the Old Head to the mouth of the previously mentioned estuary . Inside these reefs are further shoals to the east and northeast, Brean Rock and Droichead na Fían, as well as the windswept beaches of Garretstown and the White Strand. This bay is the shallowest and most treacherous in this area of the south coast and best avoided in the type of conditions that prevailed on that fateful winter's evening. An added obstacle was the wreck of the 4406-ton *Konarky* which was involved in a collision off the Galley Head in 1917 and eventually grounded

---

281   *Cork Examiner*, 22 December 1927, p.7.
282   Edward, J. Bourke. *Shipwrecks of the Irish Coast,* 1105-1993. Power Press, Dublin 1998, p.110.
283   *South and West Coast of Ireland*; Sailing Directions Irish Cruising Club. Universities Press 1993, Belfast. p39.

off the beach at Garretstown, and whose remains break the surface at low water to the present day. Before the *Pearl* grounded she would have been perilously close to this hazard.[284] Because Captain Gordon did not frequent this coastline, the chances are that he did not have suitable charts for the area. However, it would have been evident to him that he was in grave danger by the time he caught sight of the west side of the Old Head. An immediate assumption to many not familiar with this area of the coastline would be that one would could have sought shelter in Holeopen Bay West, immediately north of the Old Head. However, this is not possible as the Old Head does not protrude straight South but south-southeast, a direction very close to the wind (southeast) that evening, thus affording no shelter in that bay. The confusion arising from this event can be attributed to newspaper reports suggesting that the wind was easterly. If it was, the vessel would have found shelter in the aforementioned bay and not ended up on Garretstown Strand. To a newspaper reporter, the small detail of a forty five degree difference in wind direction may seem negligible; however, to a mariner it changes the whole complexion of the story. It may be that coastal people refer to winds collectively as easterly if coming from that direction for a sustained period of time, despite the fact that the winds may have varied between northeast and southeast. It is a small detail but a crucial one in this instance. The *Cork Examiner* of the period does not name any of the reporters and questions must be asked as to how accurate these reports are.

The first report of a vessel in distress came on the night of 19 December and it was reported in the *Cork Examiner* the following day.

> An unknown vessel, stated to be a schooner, was wrecked off the Garretstown Strand, near Kinsale, about 7pm last night. It is believed that all hands were lost. Shortly after seven o clock the attention of residents near the strand was attracted by eight signals from a steamer, apparently about a quarter of a mile away. There was a very rough sea running and it was impossible to see more than a few hundred yards owing to the darkness.[285]

In the same edition, Denis Healy of Garrylucas said he saw the vessel hove to off the Old Head earlier that day (probably head to weather with a sea anchor out would have slowed down the drift of the vessel). It could also have used a drogue over the stern to slow down the way made by the vessel.

The report from the above newspaper continues to say that the civic guards from nearby Ballinspittle village were amongst the first visitors on the scene and they pointed their motor car lights seaward in an attempt to aid the rescue. At this point, the coast guard service from the Old Head had also arrived on the scene, the station being one and a half miles distant from the scene of the grounding. Cries could be heard from the vessel which had grounded on a shallow reef in the northeast corner of Garretstown Strand and, according to reports from the same source, some members of the crew could be seen clinging to the mast. Two rockets were fired, but to no avail as the vessel was soon lost to sight from those on the shore. Wreckage was washed on to the strand within half an hour, confirming the worst possible outcome.

284 Edward, J. Bourke. *Shipwrecks of the Irish Coast,*1105-1993, Power Press, Dublin1994. p.120.
285 *Cork Examiner*, 20 December 1927, p.7.

'A letter retrieved from the debris, confirmed that the captains name was Ernest Gordon, however the name of the vessel was not mentioned'.[286] The Courtmacsherry lifeboat was thought to have left for the scene of the wreck at approximately nine o clock, however in such severe a case of weather it would have been of little assistance. The report goes on to state that 'such was the severity of the tempestuous conditions at sea last night was shown by the fact that three Cove-bound liners were delayed and not expected in until tomorrow night'.[287]

The reports in the *Cork Examiner* of the following day, Wednesday, 21 December, shed more light on events, with the vessel being identified as the *Pearl*, a schooner registered at Gloucester in England.

At this point in time the collier was a total wreck, with the shell of the hull thrown up on the northeast corner of Garretstown Strand. 'It was initially thought that the vessel, a collier, was bound for Kinsale with coal for a local merchant, but on enquiry the merchant stated that this was not so. By an amazing coincidence a cargo of coal which had been consigned to him from England went down with a steamer named *Jane* which was lost in the Mersey with all hands, it is believed last Saturday'.[288]

It was reported in the same article that the lifeboat from Barry's Point searched the area on Tuesday, 20 December, to no avail. The story connected to events of the day was told by Mr John Morgan, superintendent of the Lifesaving service at the Old Head. He stated that:

The news was first related to him by Denis Healy who lived in the vicinity of the shipwreck. Low tide and a lull in the gales made it possible to visit the wreck on Tuesday, what remained was a badly holed hull with an intact bowsprit; all other attachments had been stripped by the elements. The coastguard confirmed that two rocket lines were fired when the vessel first foundered, the second reaching the mast of the ill-fated vessel, where the crew were seen to cling to, however the mast parted from the vessel moments after this and the victims were seen no more. A large group of people witnessed this scene, thought to be in the region of three hundred, along with the coast guards and civil guards from Ballinspittle, as well as Clonakilty and Bandon.

The following day, Wednesday, 21 December, saw the sea return its first victim. At ten fifteen that morning, Mr Barrett, a farmer from nearby Bogstown, found a body in a cave a quarter of a mile west of the wreck site, identified as being an Oriental man. A short while later, at twelve noon, a second body was retrieved from the same spot. This victim was described as European, with about five day's growth of beard. From the elderly and well-nourished appearance of the man, it was thought that this may have been the captain.[289] Much commentary on that day's publication is given to weather conditions which prevailed throughout the north-east Atlantic from the end of October until late December, with reports of foundering, delays and structural damage. In those two months, one hundred and twenty people were rescued by lifeboat services throughout the British Isles.

286 Ibid.
287 ibid
288 *Cork Examiner* 21 December 1927, p.7
289 *Cork Examiner,* 22 December 1927, p.7.

The same publication yields further information concerning the vessel. Additional confirmation of this came from a Captain Nolan of Skibbereen who identified the body of Captain Gordon following a description given to him by the Civic Guards. Captain Nolan was a friend of the late Gordon; he also confirmed that the vessel carried a crew of four apart from the captain. Nolan confirmed that the vessel's usual trading route was from the clay china ports of Cornwall to the Mersey. He believed she was hundreds of miles off her usual course.

The same Captain Nolan is mentioned again on the *Cork Examiner* of Saturday, 24 December. A prominent Cork shipping agent stated he thought the schooner was light on her last voyage, as the quantity of coal found in the forepeak of the wreck was only about as much as would be needed for use in the galley. He believed that, in making her short trip in the southwest of England, she got caught in the gale, which tore away the sails of Captain Gordon's schooner and, being unable to reach the Lizard Light (east of Land's End), owing to the contrary wind, was swept out of her course and made for the nearest light, that at the Old Head of Kinsale.

It seems coincidental that Captain Nolan's experience gives us some clue as to what may have initially led to the *Pearl* ending up at Garretstown. He experienced his own hazardous crossing at approximately the same time. This is recounted in the *Cork Examiner* of Saturday, 24 December 1927. What follows is a summary of the experience of Captain Nolan's schooner, the *Loch Ryan*, in the same area, in the days prior to the grounding of the *Pearl*:

Captain James Nolan, a native of Skibbereen, came from a prominent seafaring family. He was owner as well as captain of the *Loch Ryan*, of which the registered tonnage was 165, and carried a crew of four. On 14 December, the *Loch Ryan* left Kinsale with a cargo of oats bound for London. For the first few hours of the voyage the weather was described as moderate freshening to a gale. However, on the following day the weather he encountered was the worst he had experienced from that direction in several years. About 10 pm on the night of Thursday 15, the fierce southeasterly winds buffeted the vessel when she was nearing the Scilly Isles. The gale rapidly grew more severe, and mountainous seas washed the schooner from stem to stern for several hours. As the winds reached storm force, they ripped her head-sails to ribbons and swept them away. Fortunately, the vessel did not turn over and no damage was done elsewhere. While the storm continued unabated, the two masted schooner rode at its storm anchor for 19 hours. The captain decided there was no prospect of improvement and decided to run for home by using the vessel's auxiliary motor, as it was impossible to proceed against the weather and seek shelter at the Isles. At 3.30pm on Friday 16, the vessel ran before the following sea homeward bound; at 6.30pm the same evening they encountered another schooner whose sails seemed to be gone, approximately 80 miles southeast of Ballycotton Lighthouse. She was showing flares and distress signals, but two trawlers were standing by. It was impossible for Nolan's vessel to assist owing to their own semi-helpless condition. The *Loch Ryan* made the safety of Cork Harbour at 6pm on Saturday night. Captain Nolan knew the vessel in distress was a schooner; however, he did not think it was the *Pearl* as the trawlers would not have left her to her fate. Captain Nolan had known Captain Gordon as he had frequently met him in broker's offices, and believed Gordon was in command of the *Pearl* for three or four years'.

The first inquest held at Ballinspittle on the 23 December was conducted by Timothy T Lucey, solicitor, of Macroom, in connection with the bodies found.[290] No definite evidence of identification of bodies was forthcoming at this point in time. One body was European and the other Oriental, and it was thought the European was Captain Gordon whose wife was on her way to Ballinspittle. The jury found a case of accidental death and commended the rescue services for their efforts. The inquest findings regarding the appearance of crew on the vessel when she grounded differ from the original statement. The original statements taken on that fateful night state that it was observed that crew were seen clinging to the mast when the second rocket was fired and that their screams could be heard. However, at the inquest on the above date, a witness stated that he thought there was no one on board. He did not see or hear people on the mast. He could see the mast, and there was something on it, but in his opinion it was the remnants of a sail and not the figures of men.[291]

It seems the cries heard came from the multitudes who gathered along the shore. To have heard any noise distinctively in such conditions at 250 yards would seem a remote possibility.

The coroner also was assured that to launch a rescue vessel in such conditions was impossible.

The widow of Captain Gordon arrived from England and identified the remains of her husband. A young woman, the mother of six children, she was poorly dressed and had not seen her husband for twelve months as the train fare from her residence to the ports was too high. She sat next to the coffin weeping. Later on that night a farm cart arrived slowly into the village with another coffined body, an Oriental of about 19 years of age, the body not as disfigured as Gordon's.[292]

Three days later, on 26 December, the body of a mixed race sailor named Monashire Richards was washed up on the shore. The inquest into his death was held the following day.

Records of the fourth missing crewman are somewhat confusing in that the *Cork Examiner* of 27 December named the final missing crewman as Reginald Cooke of Runcorn, Cheshire. However, in the 14 February edition of the same newspaper, the day after the body was recovered, they name the fourth victim as Wesley and not Cooke. The body was found in a badly decomposed state on the White Strand about a

290   *Cork Examiner,* 24 December 1927.
291   Ibid.
292   Cork Archives Institute, *Breathnach Papers,*pr24(27)box 4(8),

half a mile south of the wreck area. The victim's address at the time was unknown and a verdict of accidental drowning was given.

This is further commented upon by a British source. It states:

> Reginald Cook, 21, of Runcorn was not found, so far as we are aware.[293]

Were Cook and Wesley one and the same person? Further investigation is needed to resolve that question.[294]

> The body was brought to Ballinspittle and in accordance with procedures was handed over for burial. Various steps in task of internment are carried out according to unwritten law, £1 payment per man to gravediggers, a shillings worth of Jeyes Fluid, 6 shillings and 8 pence worth of whiskey and a lorry too must be paid for. The remains were interred at Old Court, on Monday afternoon.[295]

We do not have an account as to where the other three bodies were interred. It is quite likely they were also interred in Old Court. The remains of the victims of the *Boadicea* shipwreck in 1816 were reinterred here on 31 December 1900, 84 years after being buried on the shore at Garrylucas, only a half a mile away from the site of the *Pearl* disaster.[296]

Various theories circulated during the months that followed. One that featured prominently was that some of the crew had abandoned the vessel via the ship's boat. This was found intact with three blankets found in the same area as the boat. Because Cook's body had not been found by early January, the consensus was that he had taken to the boat and that his body had not washed up in the same area as the others.[297] This sort of deduction would hold little water in today's world, and it is difficult to evaluate how that idea was accepted at the time.

In an interview, a well-known yachtsman of the time, Mr H.P. Donegan, a solicitor, disagreed with this theory, on the grounds that it was impossible for a short-handed crewed vessel to end up in such a final position without having crew on board. He states that not having found the final crewman means absolutely nothing, and that the vessel used too much northing (went too far north) in her attempt to avoid the reefs of the Barrels and struck what he termed the 'Ducks Bridge' North of Garretstown Strand [*sic*], before grounding in the northeast corner some quarter of a mile away.[298]

293 Research@shipwrecks.uk.com
294 *Southern Star*, 18 February 1928, p.3.
295 CAI, Breathnach Papers, pr24 (27) box4 (8).
296 White, Raymond, *Their Bones are Scattered*: A History of the Old Head of Kinsale and surrounding Area, Kilmore Enterprises 2003, p.112.
297 *Cork Examiner*, 4 December 1928.
298 *Cork Examiner*, 6 January 1928. p.7.

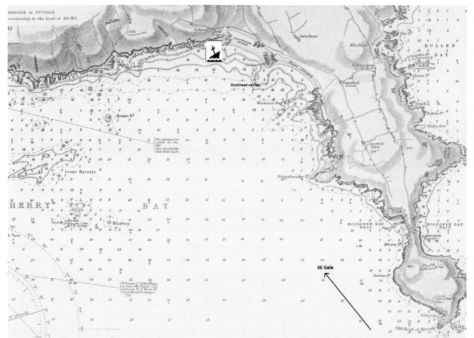

⚓ Fig.53: Chart showing the final resting place of the *Pearl* in the north-east corner of Courtmacsherry Bay. The bay abounds in shallow reefs and would be virtually impossible to sail out of in such circumstances.

This makes some sense, particularly in relation to avoiding the Barrels (the middle of the bay is very turbulent in such conditions). However, if the sail had been badly torn earlier in the voyage, how did the vessel achieve such a beam reach? He refers also to the reef called the 'Ducks Bridge'. This name I have only heard referred to by some fishermen from Courtmacsherry, the local variant in the Old Head area is '*Droichead na Fían*'. Donegan makes a common mistake that is still made today by collectively calling the White Strand (Garrylucas and Lispatrick townland) Garretstown. He says the reef is north of Garretstown, when it is actually south of Garretstown, between both beaches.

The *Pearl* of Gloucester paid a heavy price for its dependency on the use of sail. When we contrast its voyage with that of the *Loch Ryan*, we can see that the alternative, the steam moto, saved the *Loch Ryan* from a similar fate. The *Pearl* was the last vessel to founder on the shores of the Old Head of Kinsale with a loss of life; it is no coincidence that this occurred simultaneously with the development of steam and motor power. For the first time in history a vessel could put her head directly into the wind and make progress into it, a feat not possible with sail. Today, modern sailing vessels can sail very close to the wind; their older counterparts had to contend with sailing several points off the wind, more cumbersome vessels with no guarantee of avoiding disaster. The weather information that is available for this period through British and German sources makes it very clear how the *Pearl* ended up where she did. This was not evident in the newspaper reports of the day for the Irish coastline, as the wind direction given was not specific and there is no specific information on the wind directions experienced apart from Captain Nolan's statement on the conditions he encountered at Land's End. The wind direction described by the press did not tally with the vessel ending up where it did. This vital piece of weather information clarifies any ambiguity.

Point Castle: About four hours after this 250-ton Swansea-based steam trawler went aground on the rocks in Holeopen Bay, she was successfully re-floated and saved in June 1936. The vessel went ashore shortly after noon in very foggy conditions, visibility was down to a few yards. Fortunately for the vessel she went aground at low water and avoided some very sharp rocks close-by. On touching the rocks the horn was sounded for a prolonged period. This drew the attention of some locals who alerted the lifesaving service under Jeremiah O'Sullivan. The Courtmacsherry lifeboat was also called to the scene and initially failed to tow the trawler off. However the trawler's sister ship was contacted by wireless and came to her aid. Four hours into the flood tide at 3.30pm the vessel slid off the rock and steamed away.[299]

Barron of Vigo: 24 June 1938

The *Barron* of Vigo and her sister ship the *Primo* of Bouzas, were steaming to the Fastnet fishing grounds in dense fog when the *Barron*, a trawler of two hundred tons, hit the rocks at a place known locally as the *Tóin*, in Bullen's Bay, on the east side of the Old Head of Kinsale. This incident occurred at 1.20am on the last Friday of June 1938. Ten hours later, she keeled over and sank in seven fathoms of water. The crew and fishing gear were retrieved by her fishing partner who steamed home towards Vigo that night.

Initially, the two vessels were proceeding west close by each other when the crew of the *Primo* heard continual hooting from the *Barron* and knew she was in trouble. The vessels did not carry radio and the *Primo* dared not get too close to the *Barron* in case she too shared the same fate on this unfamiliar shore.

> "We did not know what had happened" said one of the crew of the *Primo,* to a press representative subsequently, "and we just had to poke around in the fog, hoping everything was all right with the *Barron*". As long as she kept making noise we did not mind, but later that stopped and we were thinking of sending off a small boat, when the fog cleared and we saw the *Barron* lying quiet close to a big cliff.
> "She was on even keel and the sea was calm. We were relieved, I can tell you."

In contrast to the excitement and fear on board the *Primo* was the calm and lack of panic on the stricken vessel when she hit the rocks. An English-speaking member of the grounded vessel told the correspondent that everything was proceeding normally until they felt a jolt when they hit the rock. However, it was calm and the crew knew they were not in danger. The side was torn open, but the flow of water was slow. When they started hooting, two local fishermen came alongside and the life-saving brigade came

299 *Southern Star,* 27 July 1936.

on the scene soon afterwards. After that, more small boats and the lifeboat were on standby and they worked all night transferring their gear to the *Primo*. The lifeboat was out of Courtmacsherry under Coxswain T. Bulpin; it had been summoned by the life-saving unit at the Old Head.

The first news of the *Barron* grounding was bought to the Old Head station by two local fishermen named Jim Healy and Batty O'Sullivan. While they were out fishing they heard the continuous hooting through the thick fog. Following the noise, they spotted the vessel in the poor visibility. The lifeboat came on the scene at 5 am, but their services were not required as the crew had been transferred to the partner vessel by the local fishermen. Sergeant Walsh and Guards Mahony and Murray of Kilbrittain were also present on the cliffs all night. There was early hope that the vessel could be towed off the rocks, but as the tide receded, she took a sideways position and when the tide came in she had a list to report. About noon, just as the transferring of the gear was complete, the *Barron* slithered sideways under the surface. Her stern could just be discerned above the water, but at high water she was completely covered. Soon after the trawler had submerged, the Dutch tug *Zwartzee* from Cobh appeared out of the fog and cruised around the area of the accident. They decided she was not salvageable and returned to Cobh.

Later on Friday afternoon, the twelve crew members of the *Barron,* under their skipper Jose Seoane, went on board the *Primo,* whose skipper was Elegandro Suares. All aboard the trawler were Spanish and only one had a good command of English. The Courtmacsherry lifeboat returned to her base at 7.20am.[300]

⚓ Fig.54: Scene from *An Oileáinín in* Bullen's Bay in 1938.The Spanish vessel *Barron* seen in the background. *Courtesy of Cork Examiner.*

Kensington Court: A British ship of 4,683 tons was lost when she was sunk by the U-32 on route from Rosario (Argentina) for Liverpool on 18 September 1939. She was carrying a cargo of cereals. Her last position was 51 31.14'N 08 28.88'W.[301]

Varia: A Swedish cargo vessel of 929 tons was attacked, bombed and sunk by a German aircraft in position 50 40.23'N 08 28.25'W on 10 August 1940.[302]
There are four more unknown wrecks to the north, northeast and south-southeast of this site, one at three miles to the north-northeast; one at eight miles, north-northeast; one at eleven miles bearing east by north and the last at eight miles bearing south-southeast.

Labud: A Yugoslavian steamship of 5,334 tons was torpedoed and sunk by the U-32, without loss of life, on 19 June 1940.[303] Position 51 03.94'N 08 33.76'W.

Respondo: A 209-ton British steam-trawler disappeared whilst trawling off the Old Head, cause unknown, presumed a war loss, on 11 September 1940.[304] Position 51 00.14'N 08 30.05'W.

Bass Rock: A Milford Haven steam-trawler of 169 tons was bombed by aircraft fire and sunk 23 miles south by west of the Old Head on 24 September 1940.[305]

Kilgerran Castle: A Swansea steam-trawler was sunk by German aircraft off the Old Head without loss of life, on 2 December 1940.[306]

The position for this wreck is 51.21.00 N 08.35.00 W.[307]
This vessel had regularly anchored in Bullen's Bay to clear her decks of fish and mend nets. Some of the local people went out in punts at times and traded eggs, potatoes, salted bacon and other produce for fresh fish.[308]
The following appeared in the local press in the days that followed:

> The British trawler, *Kilgerran Castle*, of 276 tons, registered at Swansea, was bombed and sunk by aircraft twenty five miles south-west of the Old Head of Kinsale, on Monday. All the crew were picked up and saved by other trawlers, which were on the scene at the time of the bombing, which occurred about 1.30 pm. The Courtmacsherry lifeboat received a call to go to the assistance of the trawler, but when she arrived the crew of the *Kilgerran Castle* had been taken on board three other trawlers, which had been standing by and which were leaving the scene of the bombing. An account of the bombing was given by the captain of a fourth trawler, who said the bombs, including, he believed, one incendiary, had been dropped by a plane. The cabin was set on fire. The trawler went full speed ahead, seemingly in an attempt to reach land, but the fire spread very rapidly and the vessel was soon ablaze from stem to stern. The last the captain of the fourth trawler saw of her was a

301 www.wrecksite.eu
302 Ibid.
303 B.T. & R. Larn, *Shipwreck Index of Ireland*.
304 Ibid.
305 Ibid.
306 Ibid.
307 www.wrecksite.eu
308 Ted Manning personal communication.

sheet of flame. When it was found that there was no chance of saving the *Kilgerran Castle*, the crew, numbering about ten, abandoned her and were picked up by other trawlers. The Courtmacsherry lifeboat was over seven hours at sea, and encountered heavy seas and very poor visibility all the way.[309]

A correction to the reported position of the fatality by the above newspaper report: The position that the vessel sunk in is approximately 15 miles south-southwest of the Old Head and roughly 4 miles from the *Lusitania*.

Mercury: A British minesweeper of 621 tons was blown up after detonating a mine off the Old Head on 25 December 1940.[310]

Juliet: A Hull steam trawler (H902). Bombed and sank by German aircraft on 20 August 1941, during passage from Milford Haven to fishing grounds 30 miles south of the Old Head in position 51 12.82'N 08 32.23'W. All 11 crew were rescued.[311]

Caliph: A 226-ton Milford Haven trawler with a crew of eleven was sunk about 12 miles south of the Old Head on 2 November 1941.

> When about 11 miles south of the Old Head of Kinsale, this trawler was attacked by German aircraft which caused her to leak, and after about thirty minutes steaming, during which time she covered four miles she was abandoned, and sank 15 minutes later. Her crew were saved, but one member died in hospital.[312]

This wreck is the nearest to the *Lusitania*, lying in 50 fathoms, about 0.75 miles southeast of that wreck in position 51.24.42 N 08.32.04 W. This shipwreck was barely discernable on the echo sounder 15 years ago and it is possible, given further deterioration, that it is now not evident.[313]

Some shipwrecks that are not evident on the bottom and are for a long time flattened are sometimes found during slack water (the end and beginning of the tide cycle before the tide starts to flow) when shoals of fish, mostly black or white pollock, congregate around the debris.

Iwate: A 314-ton British trawler, which had previously been attacked by German aircraft three times in 1940 and survived, was lost 25 miles south of the Old Head on 1 May 1946. It was presumed she detonated a mine.[314]

---

309   *Southern Star,* 7 December 1940, p.9.
310   B.T & R. Larn, *Shipwreck Index of Ireland.*
311   www.wrecksite.eu
312   B.T & R. Larn, *Shipwreck Index of Ireland.*
313   Shane Murphy personal communication.
314   B.T & R. Larn, *Shipwreck Index of Ireland.*

Fils de la Tempète: 23 March 1958

On the Sunday night of 23 March 1958, the French trawler *Fils de la Tempète,* while attempting to take refuge in Kinsale from a fierce south-easterly gale, mistakenly ended up on the shore at Bullen's Bay. The vessel's plight was observed by Jimmy Nyhan of Dooneen Lower who resided close to the shore on the north-west corner of the bay. He raised the alarm. Meanwhile, a distress signal sent out on short range radio was picked up by Seamus O'Neill, shipping agent in Kinsale for the French fleet and a fluent speaker of that language. He alerted the Courtmacsherry lifeboat and the new lifeboat put to sea immediately. Fortunately, assistance was not needed as the seven members of the crew were hoisted ashore by the Old Head life-saving group who made their way to the Speckled Door licenced premises owned by Mrs May Lordan of the Old Head. All seven were shocked, soaked and exhausted, some of them being clothed only in pants and sweaters. Dr John O'Donovan of Ballinspittle examined all of the crew who escaped with little more than a few scratches. They were taken by motor car to Dempseys Restaurant in Kinsale where they settled down for the night. The crew were as follows: Jean Morzadee, skipper, aged 38, married with two children; Alain Lucas, mate, aged 44, married with two children; Alain Charot, engineer, aged 51, also married with two children; Rene Lubee, aged 32, married with four children; Bernard Pierre, aged 30, married with two children. The two other crewmen, Jean Leraun, aged 26, and Jean Calvez, were both unmarried.

⚓ Fig.55: The French trawler *Fils de la Tempete* was lost in the inlet on the north side of *Pointe Cléire* on the left foreground of this image, marked by a red star. The fishing vessel Macks was lost in 1910 on the top right hand corner of image. The Speckled Door public house and the adjoining pier are in the top background of image. The strand in the centre is Gravel Strand, the headless body of German airman was washed ashore here during WW II. *Courtesy of Kevin Dwyer.*

In the course of an interview, the skipper told a press conference that the vessel and her sister ship, the *De La Paix,* were putting in for shelter. Since he had visited the port a few weeks earlier, he was acting as guide. He somehow missed the Bulman light at the mouth of the harbour, went off course and ran aground. The *De La Paix,* on being informed that the others had been saved, proceeded into Kinsale where she tied up alongside twelve other French trawlers in out of the weather. The Courtmacsherry lifeboat made for home but, because of the southeast gale blowing into the bar, they could not enter the harbour. They waited outside for enough water to enter later on that day. The lifeboat crew consisted of J.Barry, Coxswain; P.Keohane, second Cox; P. O'Neill, engineer; B.Madden, bowman; E.Fisher and D.Lawton.

During the night the *Fils De La Tempete* was dislodged because of the high waves breaking incessantly over her. When morning came, she was lying broadside across the stony inlet, just on the northern side of *Pointe Cléire* with her back broken, badly holed in several places and her bottom practically gone. She was a total loss. The vessel was owned jointly by skipper Morzadee and his sister. Her value was placed at £15,000.

When the skipper and crew visited the site on Monday, they found that their vessel had been ransacked during the night. Apparently, some persons lowered themselves on a rope down the sheer drop of fifty feet to the vessel and, getting on board, took away personal effects, money, wine, ship's documents and the identity papers of the crew. The local Garda investigated this. The Frenchmen salvaged the echo sounder, a ship's brass clock and other valuable equipment. On their return to Kinsale, they went on board some of the French vessels and returned to France on them. Among those who paid them a visit on Monday was Captain R.Guilbourg, commander of the French Naval Fishery Protection vessel, the *L'Aigle,* which was berthed in Cork. Mr Basil Gotto, the French consul in the city, who was also the receiver of wrecks, visited as well. This official, with the consent of the revenue commissioners, administers law in relation to wreck and salvage.

The *Southern Star* reported on 29 March 1958 that the inhabitants of the area disclaim all responsibility in regard to missing articles. In an interview, Mr O'Neill said that as far as he was aware, nothing was stolen from the trawler but the ship's papers. The crew's passports and some money were missing. Most of the running gear of the ship, he added, had been taken to a place of safety with the knowledge of the Gardaí who kept a twenty-four hour watch on the wreck until insurance matters were cleared up. Today, all that remains of the wreck are the driveshaft, which can be seen at low water in the first inlet immediately north of *Pointe Cléire,* three fields east of the Speckled Door public house.

⚓ Fig.56: The drive shaft from the Guilvenic trawler, *Fils de la Tempete* is still to be seen in this stony inlet a few fields east of the Speckled Door public house. *Courtesy of Michael Prior*

Sally Brown: A 28ft fishing vessel from Kinsale was lost when she went ashore in fresh easterly conditions at Faill na Áidh, just to the north of the De Courcey castle and bawn wall in Holeopen Bay East, in 1963. The three man crew climbed the very precipitous cliffs on the peninsula to safety.[315]

⚓ Fig.57: In 1963 the *Sally Brown* was lost at the foot of these cliffs and her crew clambered up the steep cliffs to safety. *Courtesy of Daphne Pochin Mould*

315 Pat Collins personal communication.

⚓ Fig.58: The Big Sovereign /*Magairlí Na tSoibhréin,* in 1814 the *Sylvan* (red star) wedged in the channel between the two rocks and the *Nelly* (1966) was lost on the southwest corner (yellow star). *Courtesy of Kevin Dwyer.*

Nellie: This 167-ton, 120ft Dutch trawler went aground on the Great Sovereign Island on 21 November 1966. Several attempts were made to pull her off by the Dutch tug *Utrecht,* but to no avail. The tug salvaged what they could from the vessel. A local trawler, the 48ft *Ros Glas,* put two men on board and tried to claim salvage on the vessel. The Nellie's sister ship, the *Arie Dez Wan,* which was on standby, took the skipper and crew on board and left for home. The vessel was listing to starboard with her stern aground on the rock in very calm conditions.[316] After several days, the vessel slipped off the rock and sank off the southwest corner of the island

Rita Rudi: A fishing vessel of 129 tons, Z 212 registration, from Belgium was lost at position 51 01.27'N 08 30.03'W, on 21 April 1969. The crew of four were in the life raft when rescued by the *Emerald* after the vessels flares had been seen.[317]

Belrose: An angling boat caught fire and sank about four miles southeast of the Seven Heads on 15 September 1976. The two crewmen were rescued. This vessel's position is 51.31.51' N and 08.38.04 'W.[318]

Ghislane Renee: The engine room of this French trawler flooded and it sank at 51.33.29 'N and 08.10.03 'W in a depth of 48 fathoms on 13 March 1978.[319]

Blue Whale: This angling boat under Cornelius De Graff was lost when she was overpowered in very poor conditions at the top of Barry's Point on 19 December, 1981. The vessel was later recovered by Celtic Divers and brought to Courtmacsherry. The skipper's body was found inside the vessel and he was later interred at Lislee. The wind at the time was southeast and the vessel was lost in the early daylight hours. [320]

316 *Cork Examiner.* 24 November 1966.
317 B.T & R. Larn, *Shipwreck Index of Ireland.*
318 Mark Gannon personal communication.
319 While engaged in trawling around the area of this wreck in 1998 I damaged my trawl badly. At a later date I was shown on a chart by a French fisherman that this vessel had sank there twenty years previously.
320 Billy Fleming personal communication.

Ardent: The 78 ft-trawler from Castletownbere struck the Bream Rock on 5 October 1984. It sank about half a mile to the east of the rock a short time later. The vessel's trawling partner rescued the crew in calm conditions.

⚓ Fig.59: The Castletownbere pair trawler *Ardent* was lost off the Bream Rock in 1984.

Rosses Morn: Was lost when the vessel struck the shore in the vicinity of Leganagh Point on 4 February 1999. The skipper was David O'Driscoll and crewman Paddy Murphy. The deckhand was never found and the skipper was picked up in the vessel's life raft later on that day. The wreck position of this trawler is 51 34. 03'N and 08 41.83'W.

Fiona Patricia: Fishing vessel caught fire and sank at position 51 02.87'N 08 41.91'W on 17 September 2001.[321]

Further losses since that time include the 164-ton wooden trawler *Dinah B*, which was lost in position 51 23.02'N 08 42.04'W on 20 December 2003.[322]

321 www.wrecksite.eu
322 www.wrecksite.eu

Astrid: Went on the rocks inside the Sovereign Islands on 24 July 2013, and subsequently sank, with all on board rescued. She was later salvaged, but the cost of restoring her were too high and she was scrapped. The tall ship suffered engine failure en route from Oysterhaven to Kinsale and ended up on the shore in almost the same place as the *Falls of Garry* over a hundred years previously in an onshore wind. The vessel was part of a flotilla circumventing Ireland.

⚓ Fig.60: *Astrid* on the shore at the west side of *Cuas Mór* with the Great Sovereign Island in the background. *Courtesy of Michael Prior*

⚓ Fig.61: The Dutch tall ship *Astrid* on the rocks, a short distance
west of *Cuas Mór,* between Oysterhaven and Kinsale in July 2013.
Courtesy of Michael Prior

Chapter VII: Folklore, Fishing, Diving and Artefact Evidence

Most of our information about losses at sea on the Irish coastline comes from the meticulous records of the British Admiralty and Lloyd's Lists. These are often very brief, with little information on exact locations. The keepers of these records worked in offices in various parts of these islands, and their world was a very different one to the men who manned the ships and plied their trade along the coasts of Ireland. The skippers of these vessels knew the coastline well, and would have had a reasonable knowledge of the various features around the coastline. If these men had written up the reports, we would have a better idea as to where exactly these vessels foundered. However, to an official in London or Dublin, a small sunken rock on the west side of the Old Head was simply recorded as 'near Kinsale' or 'near Courtmacsherry'. In most cases, we do not have the exact location available from official records.

However, the study of placenames is often a good indicator as to tragic happenings in various places. Placenames can often be the only window of knowledge available to us about a particular place, and are a very valuable tool in the search for hidden history. The people who were the custodians of these names were very aware of exact locations, given that they rarely travelled outside their own parishes, and knew their own world intimately. This is quite the opposite to today, where people live in a global world and have largely lost that knowledge of their townland. This intimate knowledge was a huge repository of name lore or *Dinnseanchas*, as it is known in Irish. Much of the knowledge of local placenames has been lost, and with it the evidence for many happenings around our coastline. The changing of names and the Anglicisation of prominent coastal features from Irish to English has hastened this, the decline of the last vestiges of information that may be known about a specific place. In the study area of this book, we are fortunate in that many of these names have been recorded, largely thanks to people like the late Francie Dempsey of the Old Head, John Thuillier and the late Phil O'Neill of Kinsale. In Courtmacsherry, Seán De Barra and others have contributed to Éamon Lankford's wonderful collection, *Logainmneach Chorcaí,* thereby ensuring the preservation of this valuable resource. Interpretations of the names are strictly speaking not perfect. The Irish language is full of nuance and the literal translation cannot be taken for the definitive in many cases. Secondly, there is reluctance on the author's part to give the English interpretations, as this often leads to the English name being adopted and the native one discarded.

Examples of the benefit of 'the lore of names' abound. One of the most evocative has to be *Cuaisín na nDaoine Báite*, 'little inlet or cove of the drowned people'. The combination of local placename knowledge, diving expertise, folklore and history contributed to the finding of *Stonewall Jackson* at this site. This is a perfect example of this combination; not all are as revealing. The *Hercules,* wrecked in the middle part of the coastline in Courtmacsherry Bay, has a couple of secrets revealed in the placenames that surround the location, German Cove, named after Carl Kooks, the only survivor from that fatal shore. A short distance to the west is *Cuas na Marbh*, 'cove of the dead'. Is this where his shipmates were washed up? Or is it the scene of another long forgotten loss of life to the sea? We do not know, but the name gives us another bit of fat to chew on. Some are blatantly obvious, like *Leaba Loinge*, 'bed of the ship', which is a stone's throw south of the Bream Rock, along the shore; or *Scoth na Loinge*, 'rock ridge of the ship', just south of the White Strand. Other combinations of placenames and archaeology came to light some years back when the skeletal remains of two bodies were found exposed through erosion on an earthen cliff-face between two suggestive placenames close to each other, *Scoth na Loinge,* in the immediate area of the discovery, and *Leabaidh a'Bháid,* 'bed of the boat', a short distance to the south.

> Burial partially washed away by storm, exposed January 1990, on the edge of cliff at Lispatrick. Three skeletons, one on top of another, lying 0.3m-0.4m below ground level. (personal communication. Rose Cleary).[32]

Fig.62: The above image is an example of the cross pollination between name lore and archaeology. The red circle marks the rock named *Scoth na Loinge* and the white circle in the far right hand corner indicates the location named *Leabaidh a'Bháid*. This clearly suggests that one or more vessels floundered at this point. This argument is further strengthened by the fact that that the human remains of three individuals were discovered at the location marked above by a blue cross in the recent past. *Courtesy of Kevin Dwyer.*

Some of these places are illustrated in Fig 63. At *Faill na Reilig*, 'cliff of the burial ground', in Bullen's Bay, a small mound was at one time evident on the old pathway leading down to the strand below. It was said that two sailors who were given up by the sea were interred here.[324] The headland named Frower Point/*An Frómhar* is said to have its name derived from *Rinnphlúir*,'point of the flour', owing to the fact that a ship laden with flour was wrecked here.[325]

During the years of World War II, the partial body of a German airman complete with identification was washed up on Gravel Strand, at the back of the Speckled Door. He was interred at Ringrone burial ground and later reinterred in the German war cemetery in Glencree, Co Wicklow. The possible remains of a plane are mentioned further on in this chapter. However, this is mere speculation and further research would be necessary to justify such a connection.

In Irish folkloric tradition the sighting of the *Arthrach Maol,* a phantom ship, was seen as a harbinger of impending doom and was greatly feared along the south and west coast. This is a common theme in Irish folk belief; other examples include the *Bean Sidhe* being heard on the eve of a relative's death, or the *Badbh* or *Morrígan* on the eve of a bloody battle.

The area has attracted many divers over the years; this is not surprising given the preponderance of wreck sites. At *Cuas Cannon,* or Gunhole, immediately north of the Bream Rock, cannons and cannon balls lie at the bottom of this inlet and it seems likely that a warship was wrecked here. Only an extensive survey of this area will confirm this. It would seem the name of the place was in use in 1790 when the French Consul Coquebert de Montbret visited this very cove and referred to it as *Cuas Canon,*[326] which suggests the name predated his visit. Similarly, cannons and shipwreck debris are found around the eastern mouth of Sandy Cove. These were uncovered during diving operations led by Bob Gunkle over twenty years ago.

Approximately one mile north of Black Head, the ribs of an old vessel protrude from the seafloor. Here lies a vessel unknown. Some years back it was marked by a buoy and explored by a couple of local divers, who were of the opinion that it was a fishing vessel.[327]

A short distance off Garretstown Strand, the bow section of the *Konarky,* which went aground here in 1918, is still evident at low water springs in three to four fathoms of water. The shaft of *the Fils de Tempete* is still to be seen in a small inlet in the middle of Bullen's Bay. A thorough diving survey, allied with the GPS co-ordinates for fishermen's fasts (snags on the bottom), would reveal much more than we already know. Around the corner, on the west side of the tip of the head and immediately under the lighthouse, lies *Cuas Gorm*. This inlet abounds in shipwreck debris, at least two

---

324 Peggy Connolly (nee Dempsey) personal communication.
325   The Placenames of the Parish of Ringcurran. *Kinsale Historical Journal,* 1987. Phil O'Neill. p.31.
326 De Courcey's Country 1790, *The Journal of the Kinsale & District Local History Society,* vol.4, Con O'Donovan, p.46.
327 Brian Perrot personal communication.

‡ Fig.63: Placenames suggestive of vessel loss, east side of Old Head. Bullen's Bay is synonymous with the settler family of that name, who in local tradition made their living by luring unsuspecting ships into that bay and plundering them. *Courtesy of Rob Jacob*

big anchors much overgrown and camouflaged by underwater growth.[328] Following the severe winter weather of 2013-2014, it is thought that much of this debris will be more recognisable in the early part of the summer, with much of the seaweed growth having been removed by winter storms.[329] More recently, some chain and other shipwreck debris has been discovered near *Cummeradúna* to the east of Frower Point.[330] The *Glaramara* immediately comes to mind, given that it was lost somewhere in this vicinity. Further investigation is needed to clarify this. Other archaeological evidence comes from Kinsale Harbour at the north end of the yacht marina. During work on a dredging programme in March 2003, timber fragments were discovered under the supervision of Rory Sherlock. Further investigation revealed a significant shipwreck. The survey found that a wreck had been buried in stiff muds that lie just below the covering sands, the removal of which was the object of the dredging programme. The wreck site was identified over an approximately 20m by 20m area and its essential outline recorded. Pottery recovered from the wreck suggests a date of the late 16th century. The site represents an important new shipwreck discovey.[331]

⚓ Fig.64: *Cuas Gorm* immediately under the west side of the Old Head Lighthouse. There is evidence in this inlet to suggest that at least one vessel foundered here. *Courtesy of Kevin Dwyer.*

328 Ann Ferguson and Tony Twomey personal communication.
329 John Collins personal communication.
330 Greham Ferguson personal communication.
331 www.excavations.ie

Shipwreck debris as evidenced from Trawling.

51°32.50'N.   08 23.61'W (Iron)

51 31.90'N   08 31.90'W (Iron)

51 35.98'N   08 30.03'W (Iron)

51 35.03'N   08 14.10'W (Bad damage to trawl)

51 30.28'N   08 31.55'W (Bad damage to trawl)

51 29.63'N   08 26.51'W   (Bad damage to trawl)

51 26.49'N   08 33.51'W   (Lost trawl)

51 28.35'N   08 24.02'W (Bad fast)

51 26.09'N   08 32.33'W (Bad fast)

51 31.90'N   08 12.50'W (Iron)

51 30.14'N   08 17.53'W (Wreck, unknown)

51 33.17'N   08 29.18'W (Bad damage to trawl)

51 25.69'N   08 31.93'W (Bad damage to trawl)

51 31.28'N   08 21.32'W (Iron)

51 28.34'N   08 29.91'W (Par Dec, Breton fisherman's chart, meaning unknown)

51 33.40'N   08 12.08'W (Iron)

51 29.65'N   08 11.32'W (Possible aircraft, metal debris brought up in gill nets)[332]

51 20.53'N   08 26.35'W (Possible wreck)

51 24.91'N   08 41.12'W (Possible wreck)

51 24.87'N   08 40.93'W (Probably same as previous reading)

51 30.30'N   08 29.51'W (Iron)

51 37.29'N   08 28.63'W (Bad damage to trawl)

51 33.85'N   08 17.04'W (obstacle, unsure of this)

---

332   Billy Lynch personal communication.

51 37.44'N   08 22.65'W (Big Anchor)

51 34.64'N   08 22.68'W (Possible wreck)

51 34.48'N   08 16.58'W (Iron)

51 34.46'N   08 16.08'W (Iron)

51 30.25'N   08 29.13'W (Iron)

51 33.21'N   08 24.48'W (unknown)

51 28.92'N   08 30.46'W (Bad damage to trawl)

51   28.67'N   08 32.06'W (Bad damage to trawl)

51   38.97'N   08 31.80'W (Big anchor)

51   18.54'N   08 12.74'W (Wreck unknown)

51   12.30'N   08 36.80'W (Wreck unknown)

51   15.21'N   08   33.68'W (Wreck unknown)

51   11.45'N   08 17.32'W (Wreck unknown)

51   10.13'N   08 33.71'W (Wreck unknown)

51 08.80'N   08 39.68'W (Wreck unknown)

51 07.45'N   08 35.77'W (Wreck unknown)

51 11.39'N   08 40.30'W (Wreck unknown)

51 11.43'N   08 23.70'W (Wreck unknown)

51 12.23'N   08 18.83'W (Wreck unknown)

51 07.47'N   08 38.11'W (Wreck unknown)

51 08.82'N   08 37.02'W (Wreck unknown)

51 06.02'N   08 37.01'W (Wreck unknown)

51 35.92'N   08 25.18'W (A wooden wreck in a broken state. Bits of timber sometimes are found with iron nails embedded)[333]

---

333   Shane Murphy personal communication.

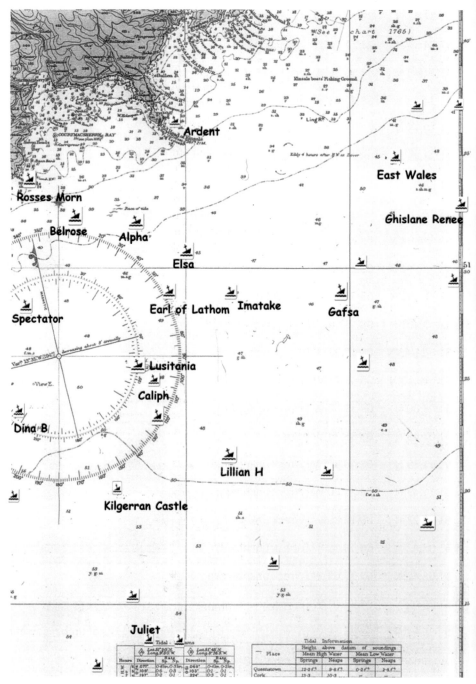

⚓ Fig.65: Chart showing the offshore wrecks in the study area. Some of the documented wrecks are further offshore and are not shown here. Most of the losses in this chart date from both world wars.

The coordinates of the wrecks listed here are the known coordinates and most probably date from the 20th century.

Many more wrecks are recorded, but their positions are not known. The offshore losses that date from before this time do not have offshore coordinates, due to lack of technology and scant reporting. The list here of trawling 'fasts' is but a sample taken from my own fishing records and the wrecks are well documented in fishermen's charts and track plotters. It is not a definitive list in any way, merely a sample. Any timber wrecks from before 1900 in an offshore context are for the most part now gone. However from time to time, samples of dowelled timber, metal, cannon and purchase blocks come up in the cod-ends of the trawl. Some of these samples are depicted elsewhere in this publication. The shells of mines are reported to naval authorities on occasion; however, this is becoming increasingly rare as time progresses from wartime events. Anchors from long-forgotten vessels are probably the most common underwater hazard encountered by trawlers working close inshore. Sometimes you can pass over them going in one direction and get snagged going along another way. These are most prevalent around the entrances of the various coastal harbours and bays which afford shelter in prevailing winds.

The reports of the comings and goings of vessels working and visiting Kinsale and Courtmacsherry give us a good indication of the amount of marine traffic that prevailed at the latter end of the 19th century. The Harbour Commissioners report for 1889 in Kinsale was as follows:

The number of vessels entering the harbour with cargo and to load was 118, exclusive of steamers carrying fish-having a registered tonnage of 11,603 tons, a falling off of nine vessels and 1,843 tons from last year, which is to be accounted for by the few vessels that arrived with Ice this season. The cargoes consisted chiefly of coal with a few cargoes of guano, three small cargoes of Ice and one of deal (timber). Of the above registered entering the harbour at Kinsale, 48 of these vessels went on to Kilmacsimon. The number of vessels outwards with cargo was 35, five less than the previous year. 31 vessels sailed on ballast. The number of boats at herring and mackerel this year was 265 of that 44 were Scots. Of these vessels 39 belonged to Kinsale, bringing the total number of fishing boats to 304. The number of steamers conveying fish during the season was 11. (Joseph Thuillier, chairman).[334] The records of the Courtmacsherry Coastguard station in 1836 state that there were 1370 men making their living, wholly or partly, from fishing. In addition, it had a small trading fleet comprising of five vessels of one hundred tons and two vessels of ninety tons. Each made eight trips annually to England, importing 8,000 tons of coal. Timber, salt and iron were also imported.[335] The tsunami that followed the Lisbon earthquake of 1755 resulted in the silting of the Arigideen estuary. This marked the eclipse of Timoleague as a port and the rise of Courtmacsherry as an alternative.[336]

334   *Minute Book,* Kinsale Harbour Commissioners from November 2nd 1870-8th July 1890.
335   *Step back in Time in Courtmacsherry.* Courtmacsherry Harbour Lifeboat Station History Group. 2014.
336   Ibid, p.86.

⚓ Fig.66: Deadeye and other wooden artefacts from old wreckage in 19 fathoms, approximately 1.34 miles south-east of the Bulman buoy, in position 51 39.05'N 08 28.46'W *Courtesy of Shane Murphy.*

Conclusion

In recent times, shipwrecks are the exception rather than the norm. This is primarily due to advances in technology, vessel construction, weather forecasting and other factors. The reasons given at inquests for losses at sea in the past are for the most part unusual today. The wrecks covered in this work are but a fraction of the overall casualties. Due to the absence of substantial records my accounts do not involve incidents prior to the mid-17th century. However, given that this area was a shipping highway (known today as the western approaches), and a gateway to the new world, it is little wonder that it abounds in shipwrecks. Other factors include its proximity to Cork Harbour, a very busy port in the past and a stage stop for many transatlantic vessels. In many of the instances in this publication, ships that came to grief were going or coming to this harbour. Many ships passing the southwest coast of Britain were often blown off course in the days of sail and ended up on our coastline in extreme easterly and south-easterly conditions. Allied with crude sailing technology and an inability to sail close to the wind, many of these ships ended up on our shores. The perilous seabed topography, Courtmacsherry Bay in particular, also exacerbated the potential for accidents to occur, evidenced in the cases of the *Guelph* and the *Pearl,* which both foundered in such circumstances. With the beginning of the industrial revolution and the advent of steam ships, losses at sea decreased. The outbreak of World War I changed this, after which losses decreased once more, only to increase again during World War II. From 1946 onwards, losses at sea reached a new all-time low and this has remained the case up to the present day. The *Honeydew* tragedy of January of 2007, in which Kinsale Skipper Ger Bohan and crewman Tomasz Jagly were lost near Mine Head, brought to local people's minds the effects of a disaster at sea on a local community. Prior to middle of the 19th century, shipwrecks were such a common occurrence that they rarely made the news. Most were reported retrospectively as the scenes of such occurrences often happened on remote coastlines. It was often several days before an account of these happenings were reported. Uncovering local lore on such matters requires consultation with as many people as possible. Some may only have a very small bit of information, others much more. However, when all the parts are put together, they contribute to the overall picture. Some of the larger vessels lost on the shore remain long in folk memory; however, most are forgotten after two or three generations. I would hope that this work would bring these stories back to life and encourage others to further research this area through the disciplines of archaeology, public records, old press reports and placenames. The south and southwest coasts of Ireland are a particularly rich research ground for this.

Bibliography

Newspapers

Cork Examiner.
Cork County Eagle & Munster Advertiser.
Irish Times.
West Cork Eagle and County Advertiser.
Southern Star.
Freemans Journal.
Cork Constitution.
Cork Mercantile Chronicle.

Journals

Journal of the Cork Historical and Archaeological Society.
Journal of the Cobh Historical Society.
Journal of the Kinsale and District Historical Society.
Mizen Historical Journal.
Sea Breezes Publications Ltd.

Books

Bourke, E.J. *Shipwrecks of the Irish Coast,* Vol 1, 1105-1993. Dublin 1994.
Bourke, E.J. *Shipwrecks of the Irish Coast,* Vol 11, 932-1997. Dublin 1998.
Bourke, E.J. *Shipwrecks of the Irish Coast,* Vol 111, 1582-2000. Dublin 2000.
Corporation Book of Kinsale.
O'Donovan, D. *Ballinspittle & De Courcey Country:* Historical Landscapes, Wordwell Ltd, Bray, 2003.
O'Donoghue, B. *Parish Histories & Placenames of West Cork.* The Kerryman Ltd, Tralee 1986.
Hepper, D. *British Wartime Losses in the Age of Sail,* 1650-1859. Rotherfield: Jean Boudriot, 1994.
Hickey, D. & Smith, G. *Seven Days to Disaster.* G.P. Putnam & Sons, 1982.
Hurley, M. *Home from the Sea:* The Story of the Courtmacsherry Lifeboat 1825-1995.
Larn, B.T & R. *Shipwreck Index of Ireland.* Fairplay Ltd, Surrey 2002.
Power, D, et al., *Archaeological Inventory of Co.Cork,* Vol. 2., Criterion Press Ltd., Dublin, 1994.
White, R. *Their Bones are Scattered:* A History of the Old Head of Kinsale & Surrounding Area. Kilmore Enterprises, 2003.
South and West Coast of Ireland: Sailing Directions Irish Cruising Club. Universities Press 1993, Belfast.

The Mariner's Chronicle: Containing narratives of the most remarkable disasters at sea, such as shipwrecks, storms, fires, and famines, also naval engagements, piratical adventures, incidents of discovery, and other extraordinary and interesting occurrences. New Haven: G.W.Gorton, 1835.
Step Back in Time in Courtmacsherry. Courtmacsherry Harbour Lifeboat Station History Group, 2014.

Archives
Cork City & County Archives, Blackpool, Cork.
Breathnach Papers
Irish Folklore Commission, School's collection. Cork County Library.
House of Commons Parliamentary Papers: Return from Lloyd's Books of all vessels wrecked on the Coast of Ireland 1848-53.
Depositions, *Register of Examinations on Oath concerning Wrecks and Casualties on the Coasts of the United Kingdom,* by the Receiver of Wrecks for the District of Kinsale, 448th section of the Merchant Shipping Act 1884, Marine Department Committee.
Minute Book. Kinsale Harbour Commissioners from November 2nd 1870 - 8th July 1890.
Ordnance Survey Name Books (1842), Boole Library, University College Cork.
Lordan. J. *The Coastal Placenames of Courceys,* Unpublished thesis, Boole Library, University College Cork. 2012.
Brady, Karl. Historic Shipwrecks of the East & West Cork Coast. Dúchas: The Heritage Service, Customs House, Dublin 2000.
Pádraig Ó Maidín articles in the Cork Examiner, 1971.

Electronic Resources
www.coastguardsofyesteryear.org/articles.
Research@shipwrecks.uk.com
http//library.metoffice.gov.uk/record=b1352142-s1
http://www.wetterzentrale.de/topkarten/fssipeur.html
www.irishshipwrecksonline.net
www.corkshipwrecks.net   www.Irishshipwrecks.com
www.wrecksite.eu   www.Infomar.ie
www.Johncollins.ie   www.michaelpriorphotography.com
www.ukho.gov.uk   www.Irelandaerialphotography.com
www.excavations.ie

Photography and chart credits
Michael Prior
Paddy O'Sullivan
John Collins
Tony Bocking
Rob Jacob

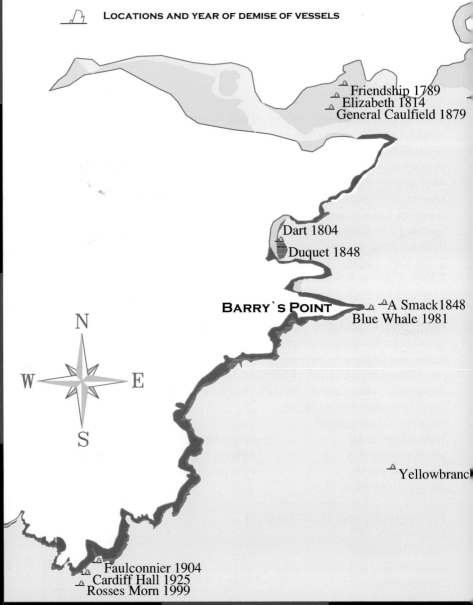

Vessels lost in the Kinsale and Courtmacsherry Bay area.

LOCATIONS AND YEAR OF DEMISE OF VESSELS

Friendship 1789
Elizabeth 1814
General Caulfield 1879

Dart 1804
Duquet 1848

BARRY`S POINT

A Smack 1848
Blue Whale 1981

N
W E
S

Yellowbranc

Faulconnier 1904
Cardiff Hall 1925
Rosses Morn 1999